There's
FREEDOM IN
Your TRUTH

THERE'S FREEDOM IN YOUR TRUTH

MILLICENT BRANHAM

XULON PRESS

Xulon Press
2301 Lucien Way #415
Maitland, FL 32751
407.339.4217
www.xulonpress.com

Unless otherwise indicated, Scripture quotations taken from the King James Version (KJV)–*public domain.*

Printed in the United States of America.

ISBN-13: 978-1-54565-976-2

TABLE OF CONTENTS

Acknowledgments vii

Preface xi

Chapter 1: Family 1

Chapter 2: Family Feud and Death in the Family 9

Chapter 3: The Maid 17

Chapter 4: New School 25

Chapter 5: Hidden Facts 30

Chapter 6: Betrayal 41

Chapter 7: New Job, New Friendship, and Family Drama . . . 56

Chapter 8: Moving to the United States 66

Chapter 9: Baby on Board 76

Chapter 10: Try to Make It 90

Chapter 11: Unbreakable 99

Chapter 12: Moving Toward the Future 165

ACKNOWLEDGMENTS

First and foremost, I would like to take time to give thanks to God for giving me strength, mercy, and guidance, and for showing me His love, mercy, and patience, as well as for guiding me through every day of my life. Second, I would like to thank my mom and dad, who have passed away. I know you are looking down and smiling at me. I want to thank my wonderful son and the love of my life, Matthew Atiogbe, whom I love with all my heart. My best friend, Steven Abranham, has been there for me no matter what; you have supported me throughout my life. I would also like to thank Sonia Danquah for supporting me when I came up with this wild idea about writing this book. I call my dear friend Kwame every day to talk, and he listens to me without judgment. My adopted mom, Vicky Crowe, you has helped me through some of my most difficult times with my son and has always been there to listen and love us; thank you. Asha Nathan, thank you for being my friend and for always being there for Matthew and me; you are an amazing person.

I met one of my favorite people in the world, Nicolle Jones, two years ago in the Atlanta airport; you talked my head off, but I'm glad you did. Thank you for being such incredible friend, and thank you for not judging me and for accepting me for who I am. Thank you for listening to me even though I know sometimes you have hard time understanding me; you have no idea the what words are coming out of my mouth, and you still listen, and for that, I thank you. To Shenorah Williams and Anne Juliette, thank you for your love, friendship, kindness, and support; I couldn't have done this without you two. To Sakyiwa, thank you for taking me under your wings and taking care of me when I was pregnant with my son; you're my real sister. Esada Manjic is the best teacher; thank you for your love and support and the fact that you continue to check on me every day.

DEDICATION

To the foreign woman who can't speak English well yet,

To the woman who was raped and ashamed,

To the woman who lost both parents,

To the woman who wasn't heard,

To the woman who almost lost her life,

To the woman who no one believed or trusted,

To the woman who has been hurt,

To the woman whose heart has been broken,

To the woman who has been treated like you are nobody,

To the for the woman who has been rejected by a man, friends,
loved ones, sisters, brothers, family, mother, and father:

*Know God sees every tear, heartbreak, worry, pain, sickness, sadness,
and injustice you are experiencing in your daily life. Have confidence
that at the right time, He will bring complete restoration to your life.*

We are strong women because we know our weaknesses. We
are beautiful because we are aware of our flaws. We are fearless
because we have learned to distinguish illusions from reality.
We are wise because we have learned from the mistakes we've
made. We are lovers because we have felt hate, pain, heartbreak,
and sadness.

PREFACE

I was born and raised in Accra, the capital of Ghana in West Africa. Everyone knows you there, and you know everyone else.

My legal name is Millicent Branham, but people call me Millie. My birth name was Stella Sourm Teye. I changed my name when I moved to the United States of America and became a citizen. I did not bother to change my name back home, since most of my family and friends still call me Stella. My father said I was born in a Catholic hospital where I received my name. I was named after the Roman Catholic sister who delivered me. He also said my name meant "a shining star, fairy queen of stars." My life has been complicated since birth. Some people say I'm not a normal person, and I proceed to ask them to define normal.

We moved to a small village outside Accra called Odumase Krobo in the eastern region. Dad took me with him when he moved, and I stayed with my dad, but my mom came to visit, and sometimes Dad and I would go to visit Mom and my other sisters. When Mom would come visit Dad, they would always fight, and it was sad. I never understood why they were always fighting. Mom would be upset, and she would go back to the city while Dad and I stayed in the village Odumase Krobo in the eastern region.

At that time, you could get a beating from your elders or neighbor when you misbehaved and would still receive a beating from your parents when you got home and they heard about your beating. It was a time when teachers would whip you when you failed your exams or misbehaved. This was a time when everyone treated each other like family. It was also a time when we would go outside and play on the streets, hunt for fruits and birds, kill lizards for no reason, build dens, and role-play as Mom and Dad. We killed crickets with empty milk cans, played hide and seek, gutter raced when it rained, and jumped in the puddles to get in the mud. Then we had to be home before it got dark.

We got dirty climbing trees and got bruises and cuts, eating mangoes and guava off the trees. We didn't have fast food, so we ate yams, plantains, and *kenkey:* corn that had been cooked and made into a ball with fish or chicken and hot ground pepper, rice, and beans. We played football called *Ampa*. There was no bottled water, so we drank water from a tap or wells. Neighbors were more family; there was no such thing as knives or guns, and church was mandatory. We watched our mouths around our elders, and we had chicken and rice, cocoa, and boiled eggs only on the Christmas and Easter holidays.

As a young girl growing up in the village, there's a tradition called *dipo* that a girl had to participate in when she entered into womanhood or before. Dad had me participating in it, and one of my cousins as well. There are a lot of girls from different houses. On the first day of the ceremony, we all entered a ritual house where our heads were shaved and our clothes were removed. We are not allowed to go home. On that day, they sat each and every one on a stool and my cousin get stuck on the stool, and they found out that she was pregnant. When you get stuck on the stool, that means you are pregnant. The next few days were hectic for my family. I was very sad because we were very close, and I wasn't sure how this could have happened. Well, maybe I should have, but I was too young to understand. They had to ban her from the village, and I never saw her again.

We had family friends in another village who did not celebrate *dipo,* and my cousin was sent there. At 4 a.m., they walked her out of the village, sweeping with a broom behind her until she crossed over to another village. My cousin was then an outcast; she had been rejected from society, never to be seen again. That day I cried so much. I wish there was something I could have done, but no one in my family would talk about it. We went back to the *dipo* ceremony.

The next day, we went to the river to bathe with calabashes. The bathing was a form of purification that cleansed our bodies and spirits. Each of us was splashed with a chalky white substance to ward off any evil spirits. We also spent time with *klami,* where our mothers, grandparents, and elders taught us crafts and traditions of *Krobo* women. We also learned how to dance, which we performed during the day of the ceremony.

We were given beads that have been passed down to our families for many generations, which represent the family wealth and social status. We were almost naked, but we wore beads from our heads to our toes. Our boobs were showing, and we walked around town just like that. Our faces were painted. There were different traditions and different activities that went on for weeks. This ceremony lasted for four weeks, and on the final day, they dressed us with *kente* and more beads. We went to house to house and danced and sat on our fathers' laps, and they put money in our mouths. Then the ceremony was over, and no one talked about my cousin.

I have never heard anything about her to this day. The *dipo* traditions continue to this day.

My name is Stella—or should I say Millie? I feel like is my duty to told my story to the world the truth that I have been raped, I have been homeless, and my family has used me more as a maid than a sister, but this does not lessen my ability or wealth as person. It will not define me, and it will not break me—not anymore. I'm not ashamed of what has happened to me over the years of my life. It is my mission to write this book to encourage other young women who have been sexually assaulted or raped by a family member or a friend or someone they trusted. They should not blame themselves for what has happened, and they should tell someone, whether they believe them or not.

Speak your truth even if no one listens to you. Your obedience is tied to someone else's freedom.

There is freedom in your truth!

For now, keep doing the right things even when the wrong things are happening. God sees everything, so stop worrying about what you have lost, who has wronged you, or what you should have been by now or how perfect your life should have been. Life is not fair, but our God is fair. God would not give you back the lost years, but He can make your future brighter than the past, and because of that, we will forget how our pasts looked. It doesn't matter what you have lost: friendship, past relationships, jobs, loved ones, family, or money. Know that God is going to bring the family you never had, the better job you never got, and the good relationships and better friendships you never had. Just keep praying to God, keep believing, keep hoping, and He will bless you and give you a better life.

It is an honor to be a survivor who is brave enough to speak the truth and not let it be buried inside yourself, forgiving no matter what. God loves you, and He has plans for your future, so don't give up on life and always put God first in everything you do. With Him, all things are possible. I'm learning to take things one day at time. I'm not perfect. I'm still making my mistakes, but I am taking them and learning from them. I was proactive enough about taking good care of myself, but I was too busy trying to do stuff. Instead of being aware in my body, I allowed stress and tension to build up, and it harmed me. I accept all this now: what I can do now, how I can allow myself to feel, and how I can avoid blaming myself in any shape or form. I have blamed myself all my life, and it is time to stop.

This book is about how to take responsibility without placing blame on anybody, some with my family, my friends and brothers and sisters. You have to take responsibility for the things that have happened and still go on with your life and take control over your life. That is the most important thing. I used to tell Jack, my best friend, that I think I am the strangest person in the world, but there are so many people in the world that there must be someone just like me who feels their bizarre flaws in the same way I do. I would imagine they must be out there thinking about me, too. I have been in Cancun, and seeing people there makes me think so many people are like some of them. They don't even have Jack to be there for them and help them when they are going through the darkest hour of their lives.

The past several years of my life have been a transitional time for me, and it has truly been a testament to the fact that I would do anything, not just for myself, but more importantly, for the love of my life: my son. I have encountered some most difficult times in my life when I couldn't see the light at the end of the tunnel, but my faith told me otherwise, and once I stopped chasing the light, I realized all along that the happiness, love, and light are internal blessings that must be discovered and shared with all those we encounter. This is my living testimony. I have been through a lot, but the worst could not defeat me. I have worked hard to give back pieces of myself through the process of writing this book with the hope that it would fulfill my goal to help other women out there in the world. I'm so proud of who I have become in this process and am beyond thankful for the love and support I received from my teachers and friends at school and the beautiful, amazing friends who have helped me.

CHAPTER 1

FAMILY

My mother raised all her kids by herself. She was thrust into the single-parent role. My mom was a *kenkey* seller (corn that had been cooked and made into a ball with fish and hot pepper). That was how Mom made money; she sold it in a small marketplace in the mornings and evenings. Mom was very hard-working. We did not have money, and we had the family together at all time. My sisters and brothers and I were together and happy. We lived in a small, wooden one-bedroom apartment with a dining room. We had two queen-sized beds in the bedroom, and some of us slept on the floor and in another bed in the dining room area, but we were happy.

Mom was a very hardworking woman. I remember a little bit about her, but not much. Mom borrowed the corn from people and turned it into corn meal. After Mom sold it, she paid the people she owed. Sometimes Mom would hide from the creditors because she didn't have the money to pay them back. When I was a kid, Mom told me to tell them she wasn't home. I remember I stood by the door and told them, "Mom is not home." I would keep looking around while I told them, and my sisters used to make fun of me about that. I remember when I was in first grade, there were no seats at school, and I would sit on the floor. I always peed on myself, and all my schoolmates laughed at me and called me names.

I remember when my sisters would carry the *kenkey* and the fish around town and sell it. That was the only way we made a living. I remember I always told on Amelie about her and her boyfriend, and she would beat me. We all ate dinner together. We did not have money, but we were all together as a family and happy.

After a while, Mom got sick. Dad and I were in the small village. I'm not sure why Mom was sick, and I don't know what made her sick. She could not go to the hospital because we didn't have the money. Mom's health was bad, and Dad thought it was spiritual, and there was nothing anyone could have done. Mom's sickness got worse with time. One morning, I was playing at my friend's house when I had this feeling. I felt something, and I knew something wasn't right, so I ran home. When I got home, my brother came from the city, and I knew then. Dad said we had to go with my brother to the city because Mom had passed away. I didn't understand what that meant, so Dad explained it. I cried and cried. The next day, we left to go to the big city. Mom was only sick for few months; when death struck, our family changed. Everything changed after Mom's funeral.

I went back to the village with Dad. I was only ten years old when Mom died. Dad used his retirement money to start a small import business, so he traveled a lot. He had his good days and bad days. Dad smoked a lot and drank a lot of alcohol, so he would send me to buy cigarettes. They sold them one at a time. I would hold it too tight in my hand, and by the time I got home, it would break into two. Dad would be so upset, and I would get the beating of my life. I didn't think Dad was a bad dad, but I would be mad and I wish I was never born. It is sad to feel like that.

I was happy when Dad would travel because I didn't want to deal with him, and each time he traveled, I would go to my second cousin's house and play with my little cousin who is two years older than me. One day, when we were playing, my big cousin said we were going to play a special game, and we couldn't tell a soul about this game. It was between us only, and I was special. My second cousin was twenty-five years old at the time. The first game started with a kiss on the lips. He made my little cousin kiss me. The second time, he made him play with my breast, which was very uncomfortable.

A few weeks later, Dad left again. I did not want to go to my cousin's house, but Dad said he didn't want to leave me alone at home, so I went. My cousin wanted us to start the game again. I told him I didn't want to, but he said if I didn't, something would happen to Dad, so I did. He made us take off our clothes and made me lie on the bed while he watched. He made my little cousin do hard sex with me, and it hurt so bad. I cried for days.

I told Dad I didn't want to go there, and he asked me why. I couldn't tell Dad why; I was scared something would happen to him. This went on for a year. I was only a kid. I wasn't sure what to do. I made a promise not to tell, so I kept quiet. After a few months, my dad had to travel again. This time I stayed home with my auntie. My aunt went to the store while I stayed home, but as soon as my aunt left the house, my cousin came to the house. This time he raped me himself. I cried and cried and stayed in my room. My aunt had still not come back from the store. After a few hours, Dad come home; something had happened, so they couldn't travel.

I was crying when Dad came home. Dad asked me why I was crying and what happened. I didn't want to tell Dad. I wasn't supposed to tell anybody, but he kept asking me to tell him why I was crying. I was shaking. I couldn't stand up and walk because there was so much blood. Dad kept asking me what happened, and he picked me up and gave me a shower. Dad said it was okay. I could tell him, and he would make it better. After he dressed me up, I told Dad that I was not supposed to tell him, and if I did, something would happen to him.

Dad said nothing would happen to him, and please tell him. I could see the sadness in my father's eyes, like he was about to cry. I think he knew what happened, but he wanted me to tell him, so I told Dad what my cousin made us do and what he did to me himself. Dad was so upset that he took his gun to my cousin's house and was going to kill him. My uncles followed Dad to make sure he didn't kill him or do anything stupid. By the time Dad got to my cousin's house, he had packed up and left town.

Nobody knew where he went after that. Dad never left me with anybody again; we went everywhere together. It was me and Dad against the world. School was far away, but some days I would take public transportation, and some days I would walk to school, which was twenty-five miles away. I had a few friends who went to the same school; we walked together, and some days I walked alone.

Dad didn't buy my clothes or underwear, so my friends' mom would give me some of their own clothes. I started to do little things like take Dad's money and use it to buy clothes and small things I needed. When he would ask me, I would lie, and Dad would give me the beating of my life. I began to be afraid of Dad. Some days

I would not go home; I would stay at my friend's house. I would do bad things and lie about it.

One day Dad traveled, and I was home with my dad's sister. I was using a small machete that belonged to Dad. My aunt came and asked me to give her the machete. I said no, and we fought over it. She cut my arms with it. There was so much blood, and I was crying and feeling alone. I went to my friend's house. The next day, Dad came home and almost killed my aunt, telling her not to ever touch me again.

I become close to Dad again, and when he traveled, he would take me with him. Sometimes I would not go to school because I was on the road with Dad. After a while, Dad didn't want me to travel; he wanted me to go to school.

Dad had a farm. We would go there together. We grew crops, such as yams, grains, oil palms, kola nuts, corn, cassava, and other root crops. Dad and I traveled miles and miles by foot to get to the farm. I liked being on the farm with Dad, and I also liked climbing trees—my favorite activity. But Dad wanted me to go to school; that was the most important thing for Dad.

I became bad, although I am not sure what to call bad. I began to steal from Dad—little things like money—and lie about it. One day, I stole $150 from Dad, and Dad had the police arrest me. I stayed in jail for one night because he said he was teaching me a lesson. Some of Dad's family members were mad at Dad for doing that. I was scared. I was only twelve years old. I felt like Dad hated me.

I know what I did was wrong, but I took the money so I could buy myself clothes. I did not have any clothes, and my friends made fun of me when I went to school. We wore uniforms, but

I wore the same shoes over and over again. I was thinking about how mad Dad was going to be, but I just wanted to fit in with my friends and not have them laugh at my clothes or how I looked. I don't think Dad understood why I did that, and I didn't understand why he had me put in jail.

After Dad had me in jail, the next day they let me go, and the police told me never to do it again. I cried on my way home, and when I got home, Dad wasn't there. He had traveled. I guess he was mad at me. We had a lot of trees at the house, so I climbed the tree, and I stayed there for hours, crying. I only came down to eat and went back up the tree. I was so mad at Dad, too. I can't believe he did that to me.

When Dad came back from his trip, it was like nothing happened. We were back to how things used to be. A few months later, Dad decided to send me to a girls' Catholic boarding school at the age of twelve. There, I made a lot of friends, and I began to be a normal person again. At school, church was mandatory. We wore white dresses to church and uniforms to class and around campus. We said our prayers three times a day: breakfast, lunch, and dinner. You had to eat all your food; nothing was to be left on your plate, whether the food was good or not. Sometimes I put my food in a paper napkin and threw it away.

Summer came, and Dad came to pick me up from school. I was so happy. Sometimes Dad and I would sit under the tree by our house and watch the sun go down. Sometimes we would sit and watch the stars, and Dad would sing a song he made up himself about how much he missed Mom. Once he told me a story about a monster with one eye and one leg who hides in the forest and catches children. Dad also said he was friends with the first president of Ghana, Dr. Kwame Nkrumah. He showed me pictures of them together. Dad was police officer for many years before I was born.

Dad told me about his childhood. He said in those days, they went to school barefooted, and they carried their books on their heads. Dad said the school was on top of a mountain, and they walked miles and miles just to get to school. Dad said they only had one meal a day—sometimes two meals if they were lucky. Dad had three brothers and one sister who didn't like each other very much and were always fighting about something. I remember my grandmother from when I was five years old. Dad's mom was a very sweet lady and kind; she took me everywhere. I remember I used to go to church with her, but she died when I was six years old.

I remember when Mom was alive, she and Dad always fought. I'm not sure why they fought, but my sisters told me Dad used to have a lot of women, and even though when Mom said something about it and he would beat her up, she still stayed with him. I said maybe she loved him, and that was why she stayed, but love shouldn't hurt that much. Love should be kind and sweet as the years go by. I think Dad had changed. The way he talked about Mom showed he really loved her. I missed her, too. I remember when I was little, I used to have lice on my hair, and she would put towels on my head and use her mouth to break the lice into pieces.

School was almost over for the summer, and I could not wait to go home. All I could think about was Dad. I wasn't doing so well at school, and I missed Dad. I was scared that he would die before I got home. We didn't have cell phones, so there was no way to get hold of him in those days. You could only write a letter to someone if you wanted to talk to them. We lived in a small village, and we didn't have addresses to send letters to. I wasn't sure if Dad was picking me up from school, but to my surprise, he did. When Dad picked me up, I was excited. I couldn't wait to spend time with Dad, but things did not turn out the way I hoped they would.

After getting home, things were different with Dad. He had changed, and he wasn't the same person I knew before going to school. He looked angry, sad, and bitter. He wasn't a happy man. I know I was sad because I was looking forward to spending time with Dad like in the old days. A few days after I had been home, I noticed Dad was drinking a lot and smoking five packs of cigarettes a day. Dad's business wasn't going so well. After a month, Dad was so drunk that he fell and broke his knee.

One of our family member came to get me, and I went to help Dad home. He couldn't walk. Back in those days, each time you saw a doctor, you had to pay out of pocket. There was no such thing as insurance, and the doctors would not see you until you paid. We didn't have the money, so Dad never went to the hospital. They did home treatment, but it didn't seem to be working. However, Dad was a fighter, and he would not give up.

Dad never remarried. It had been always Dad and me, but it had not been the same for Dad. He missed Mom so much, and it put him into depression and drinking. It had been hard for me too, but we had each other. I was still young, so I didn't know about life. I was scared that I would lose Dad, too. Dad and I always slept on the same bed. I never saw anything wrong with that, but my family hated the idea. It didn't matter to Dad, though.

CHAPTER 2

FAMILY FEUD AND DEATH IN THE FAMILY

My uncles and aunties didn't like me very much. I kept thinking that maybe I was a troublemaker. I didn't get along with any of my family for whatever reason, and it really didn't matter to me because I had Dad. I kept praying and hoping that he would get better soon. I would cook clean and change Dad's clothes because Dad became very sick. I was worried about him. I didn't want to go back to school, but Dad said I should go. Dad had a friend whose name was Mason, and he had a friend at the other side of town, so he took me there so I could meet her.

The woman's name was Ava, and she had one son and a daughter whose names were Duke and Sue. Duke was very handsome guy. I had a crush on him. We all went to the same school, but I was at the boarding house, and they were not. Dad's friend wanted me to stay with them just in case Dad couldn't pay for my fees at the boarding house. They were very nice and welcoming. I liked them a lot, especially Duke. They told I could come back and stay with them. I said okay. Meanwhile, I was worried about Dad being sick. I didn't want to leave him alone. I had grown up fast. I didn't even enjoy being a kid. In fact, I had never known how it felt to be a kid because I had been through a lot as a child.

Back to school time came, and Dad was able to send me to school. While I was at school, I was worried about Dad because he couldn't come visit. He was getting worse every day. I would stay with Duke and his mom sometimes, and sometimes I stayed at school. I was happy to be around Duke because I liked him. We became close. Duke's grandmother said that was too bad, because Duke wanted to be a Roman Catholic father.

We all went to Catholic church, but I was hoping that one day he would marry me. I was thinking that he liked me, too, by the way he looked at me. I was not sure what love felt like, but I felt something inside each time I saw him. We both looked at each other, and I thought it was a great feeling.

Meanwhile, it had been two years since Dad became ill, and he was not getting better. He did not come visit this time. I couldn't wait to go home, but when I got home from school, Dad couldn't walk. I had to take care of Dad, give him a shower, dress him, feed him, and help him use the restroom. I was fourteen years old at the time, and every time I went back to school, I was worried. I was no longer happy. I kept things to myself, didn't talk much to my friends anymore, and became shy around people. A few months before my fifteenth birthday, I came home from school and Dad wasn't looking good. None of his family cared about him, so at almost fifteen years of age, I was still taking care of Dad.

Dad was my whole world. I was so afraid that he would die, and I would be left alone in this world. I would cry when no one was watching. I didn't let Dad see me cry. Dad said that everything would be okay and that I should not worry, but deep down my heart,

I was worried, thinking, *He is all have. What am I going to do if Dad dies today? Who would take care of me?*

I asked God not to take him away from me and told Him that I needed Him to save Dad. My worst fear came true one evening. My family had a meeting, and they were discussing funeral arrangements. I went and told Dad, but he said not to worry; I would be okay. That night Dad, asked me to sleep by his side, but my aunt said no. Dad said, "Don't worry. I will see you in the morning."

Around 3 a.m., I heard Dad call my name, but by the time I got to his room, he was sleeping so peacefully. I began to wake Dad up, and I shook him, but there was no response. At that moment, I knew he was gone. I felt empty. I felt loss. I could see the room spinning around, and I immediately peed on myself. I felt sick to my stomach. I just sat on the floor by his side. I couldn't move; I couldn't talk. I felt numb. I felt completely lost and hopeless.

I had known this would happen, but what I didn't know was that it would happen that morning at 3 a.m. My whole world just ended right before my eyes. I couldn't even cry. I just sat there for hours. I'm not sure how long I sat there. At that moment, I wasn't sure what was going on. All I could see was my family moving back and forth, and people were coming in and out of the house until one of our family friends came to me and helped me up. I looked at her, and she hugged me as tears began to fall from my face.

They sent for our other family in the big city while they prepared for Dad's burial. I had a friend next door, so I stayed with them the whole time. It was really hard for me to be at the house, knowing Dad was gone. I still couldn't believe it; the next two days it felt like years. My other cousin came from the city. After two days, finally they were going to bury Dad. On the third day, they did the visitation and burial.

After Dad's funeral, I wasn't sure what is going to happen to me. The day I lost my father was the day I realized what it meant to lose control. People talk about losing control of themselves all the time, whether because of anger or drinking or losing their jobs or loved ones, but I didn't know what it was truly like to lose control. I'm not talking about my emotions, but about my life; I lost control of my life, and everything around me fell apart. I have heard people say that you can only control yourself and how you behave in any given setting, and you can never control the circumstances around you. You can't control how other people react—only how you, yourself, act.

That's a great tragedy of life: one minute everything is perfect, and the next minute is in flux because of the circumstances happening around you. It is hard when everything you have lived for is taken away from you. People say it was fate, God, or bad luck. How was I supposed to pick up the pieces of my life and move on? I was not sure how I could survive the loss of Dad. It broke me into pieces, and my heart was heavy. I lost my best friend, my life, and my world. I was not sure who would take care of me, or how my life would be without Dad. It was hard just to think about it.

I hadn't seen or spoken to my half-sisters and half-brothers in years. My third cousin took over my Dad's business, and I hoped they would use the money to take care of me. However, that was not their concern; sometimes I wasn't sure where to find my next meal for the day. Some days I would go the whole day without a meal, and some days my aunt would cook, but I only got a meal when I helped around the house by doing chores like going to the farm and bringing water and firewood home. Also, I could go hang out at my friend's house and help them cook, and I would get something to eat.

Dad's family didn't care much about my well-being; they didn't even notice if I was around or not. I was all alone with no one to care for me. I was on my own with no father or mother—no one—to care for me, but I wasn't thinking about anything but how to make my life better. I wasn't the luckiest girl on earth; in fact, I felt I wasn't lucky enough to have my family to care for me.

At the time, the only thing I could think of was Dad and how I wished he was still alive and there with me. I missed him so much. My friends and I would walk to the lake side where we would wash our clothes and dry them on the leaves. We would then take a shower, hiding in the forest, and play games after we would fold the clothes and put them in a different bucket. We would carry water back home on our heads while holding the bucket with clothes in the other hand. After we got home, we would then go back to the lake and bring more water home. Afterward, we went to the farm and brought firewood. Then we sat by the fire and began cooking.

I went back to school with no food and no money. We got breakfast, lunch, and dinner at school, but the food there was not that great. I couldn't complain at that time, but then it came time to pay my fees, and I didn't know what to do. One Sunday after church, I didn't go back to my room. I stayed at church and started crying. One of the Roman fathers whose name was Father Clement came to me and why asked I was crying. I told him that I was an orphan, without a father or a mother. He said, "You are my daughter now, and I'm your father." Father paid all my fees and paid for my food, clothes, and books.

A few weeks later, everyone was taking a nap, and I was sitting alone. I began to feel very nervous. My heart was jumping out of my chest like something was not right. That night in my sleep, I felt very cold hands on my cheeks like a touch. I used my comforter to cover my head, and I heard some of the girls talking, so I lifted my head up to see what was going on. Some of them said they heard a man's voice, and most of us woke up.

Everyone was talking, and for a second we all heard the voice again (a very deep voice that stopped talking). Everyone was so scared, and Sister Lucy came and said we should go to sleep, so we slept in twos. I recognized the voice, but I did not tell anybody. I was scared the most.

I thought if I told them, they would think I was crazy, or maybe no one would believe me, so I didn't tell a soul. I felt all alone like I was in this alone. I hadn't been to Duke's mom's house, but I saw Duke and his sister at school. Their mom was a nurse at the school, so I saw her sometimes. I wasn't sure what I was feeling and how I was doing. No one had asked me how I was doing, and no one knew my pain. One day at class, there was a lot of blood in my clothes, and it got on my seat. I didn't know what that was, so after school I covered my belt with my books, and I cleaned my seat.

When I got to my room, I took a shower. There was so much blood. I didn't know to do. I was so scared. I didn't know who to tell or ask. I didn't understand what was happening to me. When I sat down, I didn't sit all the way; I would sit halfway so the blood wouldn't go on the seat. It had been three days, and the blood was still coming. I would cry every night. I was so scared, and I kept asking myself why there was so much blood coming out of me.

The next day, the blood stopped. I was so happy. I couldn't believe it stopped. I was relieved, and I thought that I was seeing blood because of what had happened with Dad or the voice we heard the previous day. The next few days, everyone was talking about it. I didn't because I knew who that was. This happened a few times at night at 3 a.m., at the same time Dad died. We would hear the same voice, and I was the only one who knew that voice, and I still couldn't tell my friends.

At school every evening, we would go to the temple and say the rosary and pray. Then we would have dinner; the food was not good, but we had to finish the food before leaving the dining hall. We didn't have a choice.

Summer break came. I didn't want to go home, but I had nowhere to go, so I did. I was afraid to go to Dad's house, but I didn't have a choice, so I went home. One day I was sitting under a tree where Dad and I used to sit and watch the sun rise. I was crying because I missed him so much. I had so much I wanted to tell him; so much had happened. I was feeling lost and unhappy when a man came up to me and said, "I'm a friend of your dad's. We went to school together before you were born," and then the man said, "I heard he passed away. I'm sorry for your loss. Your dad loved you very much, and he is always going to be with you. There's no need to cry." The man gave me money, but as I turned my back for a second, he was gone.

I ran out of the house and stayed on the street until my aunt came home. I told her what had happened. She told me I was being paranoid. That evening, my aunt sent me to the store. Because it was a small town, there were only a few street lights. As I was coming back from the store, something told me to turn around, and there he was: Dad, standing there watching me. I immediately froze with fear. I couldn't move or run. I then peed in my pants and began to run home. I dropped everything I was holding. I went home and told my aunt. She did not believe me, so she went with me to get the stuff I dropped, but when we got there, he was gone.

None of my family believed I had been seeing Dad. I just hoped one of them would believe me. I felt alone; no one was on my side. I cried myself to sleep every night. I was scared to stay home alone, so I would go to my friend's house and hang out until bedtime. No one cared to try and find me. Every night when I would sleep, I would feel the cold hands on my cheeks. It got so that I didn't want to go home at night or in the daytime.

After I had been home for a few months, I saw blood again. I wasn't sure why this kept happening, so I would put folded paper towels in my underwear, and I would wear a short pant under my dress so that when I sat, it wouldn't get on the seat. It did not work all the time; sometimes the blood went on all over the seat and my clothes.

CHAPTER 3

THE MAID

My three cousins lived in the big city. Each time they would come to my dad's house in the village, I would clean and cook for them as though I was their maid. They didn't really care about me. Back when I was a little girl, my dad told me that Mom and he had arranged a traditional marriage for me. Back in our hometown where they would make marriage arrangements between two families, I was supposed to get married to one of my cousins, but I wasn't sure what to think of that. I don't think my cousin wanted that, and I don't think he liked me very much. I couldn't tell. Just the way he looked at me when they would come from the city and leave told me they didn't have anything for me. I would ask about Dad's business and the money, and he would say things were not going well, but I knew that was a lie.

It hadn't been easy since Dad died. I would stay with my friends next door to us, and they were very nice. I would help them clean and cook so I could get something to eat. Sometimes I would sleep in their house. It almost felt like I lived there; I would only go home if I needed clothes. I was too scared to sleep at Dad's house because it felt like I would see Dad's ghost. However, my friends would make sure I was okay.

I grew up in a small town. We would go to the lake to get water, and it was fifteen miles away. We would carry the water in a bucket on top of our heads. We cooked with firewood, so we would go to the farm and bring firewood and get water in the river. Sometimes I would go alone, which made me always look behind me the whole time because I was scared. It was quiet on the way home. I would take the bucket and put the water in it and carry it on my head. Everything was on foot. It was about twenty to thirty miles away, but I was used to it.

My aunt and uncles didn't care much about me; my aunt always accused me of stealing her money, clothes, food, and soap. Sometimes I felt like I had been cursed; nothing seemed to work out for me. I know God saw my tears; my heart broke at the pain I had been going through. I stopped going to Dad's house. I was staying at my friend's house. When I would come home from school, I stayed with my friend and her family. They loved me like I was part of their family—like I was their own. I liked being there with them.

One day, my friend told me about a church. She said the pastor was very good at what he did. He would pray for you if you were cursed. I sometimes felt I had been cursed, so we went to the church. It seemed like a good church, and they were having overnight praying. I wanted to go, but my friend couldn't go, so I went alone. The pastor took me a room alone to pray for me, but before I knew what was happening, it was too late for me. He put his hands in my underwear. I was so uncomfortable. I was a very shy person, and I didn't know what to do. He said it was part of the prayers. After he was done, I ran out of there and never went back and never told a soul. I was scared no one would believe me. I wished

Dad was alive; he would believe me. I missed Dad so much. I felt so much pain and sadness. I had nothing, and I kept hoping and praying for better days ahead.

When I got home, I took a bath. We would put the water in the bucket and stand outside when it was dark to take a shower. That night I cried and cried. I was so sad. I didn't know why all this was happening to me. I felt like I didn't like men. I told myself because men hurt me, I didn't think I would get married because they were evil. That was how I saw them. Life hadn't been easy for me. I was in this world all alone, and I felt like the world was against me.

I thought about my half-sisters and brothers, but the truth is, I hadn't spoken to them since Mom died. A few days later, I decided to go look for my half-sisters and brothers, so I left the small town to go to the big city. My sisters were very happy to see me. I said to myself, "Finally, I can breathe." Little did I know that my troubles were far from over. I stayed with my sister Kim, who is four years older than me. She was married with kids, and her husband was rich.

The first few days were amazing, and then I had to go back to school. Kim bought things I needed for school. I was happy when I got to school. My friends saw a difference in me, and my best friend said, "I'm happy to see your smile again. I thought I lost you." Father Clement continued to pay my fees and for my books. The whole school year was amazing. The end of the school year came so fast, but not fast enough for me. I had to say goodbye to my friends, which was hard. I would not be seeing them next school year because grades ten through twelve were in a whole different school.

As we were getting ready to leave, my brother John came. I was surprised to see him there, but happy at the same time. He said my sister Kim said to pick me up. My brother was rushing me, so I didn't get to say a proper goodbye to my best friend. In those days, there were no cell phones; you could only write a letter, I couldn't get my best friend's address because I had been rushed. My brother and I left.

I would have to stay home for five months before starting at my new school. The first day I was home felt great, and on the second day, when I woke up in the morning, my sister put clothes out in front of her door on the floor for me to wash. During those days, there was no washing machine; it was all hand washing. There were a lot of clothes for me to wash; it took me two hours to finish. It was hard to wash jeans with your hands, especially man clothes, but the wash also included comforters. Kim opened her back window and yelled, "Are you not done? Why are you taking so long to finish washing?" I didn't answer her; she was annoying me.

When I finally got done with the laundry, I had to mop the floors and sweep the whole house. By the time I got done with all that, breakfast time was over, and it was lunch time. After I had lunch, we would then go to the market, come back, and start cooking dinner. I didn't get to sit down from the time I woke up until the time I went to bed. After dinner was done, I would wash the dishes and mop the kitchen floor. This went on every day for five months. I felt like I was more like a maid than a sister. I didn't want to go back to Dad's hometown, so I continued to do what I had to do.

When she sometimes put clothes out for me to wash, Kim would add some of her old clothes that she didn't wear anymore and said, "Here are some clothes for you," and since I didn't have any clothes, I would accept them gratefully. Sometimes I wrote down my thoughts in a notebook and put it under my pillow. One morning, my sister Kim send me to the store, but when I got back home, I felt something was wrong. When I got there, I saw my other sister, Lisa. She was there, and they both called me and questioned me about my notebook and why I wrote such things about them. I thought that was supposed to be my safe place where my thoughts would be kept safe. I felt like I was in front of a judge. They said I was an ungrateful person and that I was taking them for granted. I told them I was sorry and it would never happen again.

Every week, Lisa would come, and so every week, I wrote my thoughts in my notebook about how I had been treated and how life is unfair. Every time I got in front of them and answered questions. Each time Lisa came to the house, I knew that I was in trouble, and each time they called me, I already knew what they were going to say. It was like I could read their minds and thoughts. I already knew what they were about to say to me. There came a time when I didn't care anymore.

I got blamed for anything that happened at the house, and I was scolded for it. Sometimes at night when everyone was sleeping, I would go outside and sit there, look at the stars, and cry, wishing Dad was still alive and thinking about how much I missed him. I began to date a guy next door, who was the first actual guy I had dated. When my sister and her husband would go to bed, I would sneak out just to hang out with him. One night, we went to the park and were walking and talking when two guys began chasing us. I wasn't sure what was going on. I thought they were after my date, so I stopped running to ask them why.

My date ran and left me behind. The guys said that we were not supposed to be there and that I was in trouble unless I gave them money, which I didn't have. They forced me and took me to their house, and each of them took turns raping me. I was on my period, but they didn't care. After hours of being raped they said, "Tomorrow, bring us money, or we will find you."

On my way home, I was crying and asking God why He had forsaken me and why all these bad things were happening to me. When I got home, my big brother John was also staying with my sister Kim, and he was standing by the gate, waiting on me. He asked me where I had been and who I was with. I told him I went for a walk, and he began to lecture me for thirty minutes. I went to my room and took a long shower and cried my eyes out. I couldn't tell anybody because they said I was a liar and a thief, and no one would believe anything that came out of my mouth.

The next day, my date came looking for me after my sister Kim went out. He asked me what happened and told me that he was sorry for running and leaving me behind. I told him I never wanted to see him again. He asked why, so I told him what happened. He said, "Let's go to the police," but I told him no and that we were done. Every day I would see him, and I would pretend as if I didn't know who he was. My brother never told my sister about me sneaking out of the house.

A few days later, my sister went out and came back with help. I thought I would not have to do the hard stuff anymore, but deep down, I knew that was not true. The next day, the new help, Amanda, and I started to clean, which made things a little easier. We mopped the floor and washed the clothes, and I dusted the house. We had a very big carpet that my sister made me clean as if I was a carpet cleaner. It took me hours to finish. It was very sad, and I still can't believe that after she brought in help, I was still doing the hard work. My soul was very sad. I missed Dad so much that I cried that night in the shower. I couldn't sleep that night.

I only had a week before going back to school, so I coped with it. Kim said to call her husband Dad, but he wasn't my dad. I did it for the respect I have for my sister and her husband. After everything I had been going through, I still gave Kim respect. I have never disrespected her in any way. I was a very shy person and very humble. I gave all my sisters respect. I put on a big smile each time; that was all I could do.

Kim's husband was very rich. He had his own business and a very big house. I respected him a lot, and I never said anything bad about him. When Kim was out of the country, I always slept with my little niece, and she always put her hands in my shirt when she slept; that's what kids do sometimes. One night, we were sleeping, and I felt a hand touching my breast, I thought it was my little niece, but when I opened my eyes, it was Kim's husband's friend who was staying at the house with us. I yelled at him and asked him what he was doing. He looked at me and said nothing and walked out.

The next day, Kim came home, and I told her and her husband what had happened the previous night. I was very upset. My sister and her husband called him, but he denied it. He said he never touched me. I screamed at him and called him a liar. I started crying. My sister and her husband said there was no need for me to yell. By the looks on their faces, I already knew they did not believe me. They thought I was making it up because when they asked him, he said nothing like that ever happened. I was very upset that they didn't believe me.

I couldn't wait to go back to school. My sister said, "It is okay. Let it go; nothing happened." I felt sad, disappointed, angry, and confused. I went into my room and cried. I was hurt; my heart hurt. I felt like my sister had betrayed me by not believing me and not protecting me. My heart was heavy. I couldn't wait to go back to school. I carried the pain inside my heart, but I tried to forget and kept moving. I kept myself busy with housework, so I didn't have to feel the pain too much.

The next few days were hard for me. I was mad, and each time he saw me, he smiled at me like nothing happened. I asked him how he felt knowing what he did; he looked at me and said, "Nothing. I felt nothing."

I said to him, "Good for you." I was so mad, but I kept my head up and I continued to do what I needed to do. Kim and her husband never talked about it or even asked me if I was okay or how I was feeling.

I guess I don't matter. I felt like it was my fault, or maybe it was something I did, or maybe I led him on somehow. I kept going through it in my mind and asking myself what I did or did wrong or what I said to him for him to try something like that. I said to myself, "Maybe I deserve it." I tried to put it behind me, but it was hard to do. I had to try; I didn't have anybody to have my back, so I let go but did not forget.

The school date arrived. I was happy and sad at the same time because I wasn't going to see my old school friends again. They all went to different schools. That morning, my sister Kim bought a few things for me for school, and I left.

CHAPTER 4

NEW SCHOOL

I had to leave early for school because I had to go to Father Clement and get my check for the school fees and books, so I took the bus and went to the missionary house. I got the checks for school, and I went to school from there. When I got to my new school, everyone came with either their moms or dads. I was the only one who came by herself; it was a very emotional day for me, but I kept telling myself to just breathe, so I kept it together. At the boarding house, they gave everyone a school mom, so I got one whose name was Mia. My first school mom didn't care much about anything. A few days later, class started. The bell rang at 4:30 a.m. for everyone to wake up, take a shower, and get ready for class. If you didn't wake up when the bell rang, the school leader would come and write you up, and also you would be waiting in line for fifteen minutes just to take a shower. There were about 250 girls in the dorm. The water was so cold in the morning, and outside it looked very foggy and very cold. The school was on top of a mountain. We all had to take a cold shower. Some people didn't take a shower because the water was too cold. We were not allowed to bring a water heater, but some of the rich kids did bring one and hid it. They got to bathe in hot water, but some of us bathed in cold water. After our showers, we got dressed and headed to the school campus. We had to be there at 6 a.m. Everyone had breakfast in a very long hall; the food was terrible, but some of us ate it. Others didn't because they came to school with provisions, so they ate before heading to campus.

After breakfast, we headed to our individual classes for eight hours. We got lunch as well. School started at 7 a.m. and ended at 3 p.m. A few weeks after beginning in the school, I made friends, and I began to like school a little more. My new friends and I skipped class sometimes and hid in our dorm room because the math teacher was very mean. He gave us assignments, and we all failed, so he beat us with a cane on our hands or backs. Each time we had math class, everyone disappeared because he hurt us. I forgot all about home because I was enjoying school more. The school didn't have water, so during the weekend, we all traveled about twenty miles to wash our clothes and bring water to campus. We carried the water on top of our heads and climbed a mountain. It wasn't easy, but I preferred staying at school to being at home.

At school, we went to church every Sunday, and we did activities. My new school was a coed school for boys and girls. The boys' dorm was ten minutes from the girls' dorm. The boys played soccer, and the girls played volleyball or hockey. I was on the hockey team, and it was fun. Being a junior at a boarding school, there was a lot of bullying; sometimes our seniors would make us dress funny and sing stupid songs and dance for them. Sometimes, we got punished and scrubbed the bathroom for a week. I had a crush on one of the seniors at school. I would pass by where he would be standing to make sure he saw me. My friends thought I was crazy and that he didn't like me, but the secret was that he did like me. He was my best friend Joy's brother.

On Sunday, church was mandatory. One Sunday when we were going to breakfast, my crush called my name. I got so excited about it that I couldn't stop smiling the whole day. The next day, we started talking. We couldn't let the other seniors know that we were talking. If they found out, I would get into trouble because I was a junior, so we hid our friendship. We would hide at the back of the school and talk; it was fun, and I liked it. I felt happy even though I was sure what I was doing was wrong. I liked the attention he was giving me.

We only had a few weeks before summer break, and I began to worry about going back to my sister Kim's house. One of my friends asked me why I was sad, and I told her. She said she lived with her dad, so I could come home with her. All my friends' families came to visit them at school, but no one came for me. I was in this world all alone and sad, so I tried to make myself happy. My friend Emma didn't make me feel left out; she always brought me around her mom whenever she came to visit her and bring her food, and she shared it with me.

On the last day at school, I left for the big city with my other friend, but I didn't go to my sister Kim's house. I went to my friend's house. Her name was Olivia. I stayed with her and her dad. They lived in a compound house. In Ghana, some of the houses were like that; the people who didn't have enough money or weren't rich lived in compound houses. The people were very nice and welcoming. Olivia's dad was very nice; they fed me and hung out with me, and we did fun things. One morning I decided to look for a job while we were home, so I got dressed and went to town, looking for a job. I went to a communication center where they did faxes, copies, and phone calls, but they didn't have anything. I was going back to Olivia's house, and I realized I lost my transportation money, so I began to walk, hoping I could get home from where I was before sundown. Home was a little far away. By car it was thirty minutes, and if I walked, it could take me about an hour to an hour and a half or more.

So, I began to walk, but while I was walking, a car pulled beside me and asked where I was going. I told him, and he said, "Get in. I will give you a ride home."

I didn't want to, but he insisted, so I got in. I realized he was going the wrong way, so I said, "That is not how to get to my house," and he said he had to be at the office, but he forgot something at home, so he would pick it up very quickly and drop me off. I said okay, but deep down, I was scared. I knew this was not going to end well.

I asked him to drop me off where we were, but he said, "Relax; I won't hurt you. I'm just picking up a file. It will just take a second." A few minutes later, we arrived at his house.

He went into the house. It took him a while to come back out, and when he did, he said he couldn't find the file that he was looking for and asked me to come in for a few minutes. He said, "I wouldn't hurt you. I have daughters your age inside," so I went in. When I got inside, there was no one there but him, so I asked where his daughters were. He said they were at school. He asked me if I wanted a drink. I said no and told him I just wanted to go home. He said, "I will take you in a minute." I was very scared at that moment. I began to feel very nervous; my heart was beating very fast like something was wrong. I just couldn't figure it out. He was in his bedroom for a while, so I went to the door to leave, but it was locked, and then he came out of his room.

I asked if I could leave, but he said no and to relax. He then began to touch me. I told him to stop, but he pulled me from the door. He then told me to be quiet and pushed me onto the floor. He ripped my clothes off. He was a strong man; I tried to fight him, beating him with my hands, but he then began to rape me over and over and over again. I was watching the top of the ceiling and thinking about Dad and crying in my head. I asked him why he was doing this, but he didn't say anything. When he got done, he told me to get dressed and get in the car. I wasn't sure where I was, so I got in the car. I cried the whole time. On the way, he said, "You are a very beautiful young lady." When we got to my friend's house, he dropped me off and said, "If you told anyone about this, no one would believe you."

When I got home, my friend wasn't there, so I took a very long shower and went to bed. My friend came home and brought dinner. She woke me up, and I told her I wasn't hungry. She asked me why I looked so sad, and I said, "I just wish my dad was here. I miss him so much and I think I should go back to my sister Kim's house and stay." She asked if she did anything to hurt me, and I said, "No, I just want to go back." So the next day, I went back my sister Kim's house. When I got there, she asked me where I was coming from. I said school, but I lied.

CHAPTER 5

HIDDEN FACTS

I tried to understand my life and why mostly bad things had been happening to me. My life hadn't been the same since Dad and I moved to his hometown. It had been one rape after another. I felt like God had forgotten about me, or maybe this was how my life was supposed to be. Some nights, I didn't sleep. I would stay up, and I would ask God to give me the strength to do what I had to do. Some days, I wished that I would also die.

Maybe I would see Dad. There was nothing else for me on this earth. I had nothing, no one to love me, and no one cared about me. I had family who thought the worst about me and who hurt me. I had nothing else to live for. Then I would hear a voice in my head telling me not to give up on life and not to give up on myself. I would feel cold air at the back of my neck like someone was standing behind me. I think it was Dad; I knew it was him. I would talk to myself, thinking he was listening. I would ask him if he was always there, why couldn't he protect from all these bad men, and if it was God and He was there, why was I suffering? Why did I have to go through hard times in life?

A month after I got home from Olivia's house, I got very sick. I couldn't wake up in the morning to do any housework, and my sister asked me what was wrong. I told her I wasn't feeling well. She went to the pharmacy and got me medications, but after a few days, I wasn't getting any better, so my other sister, Lisa, came. They both asked me if I had my period. I told them no; they asked if I had a boyfriend, and I said no. They didn't believe me.

The next day, my sisters took me to the hospital, where the doctor told them I was pregnant. When we got home, they questioned me for hours. I just looked at them; I guess that is what sisters do when they care about you. I still couldn't tell them. They were very disappointed in me. I didn't tell them because they wouldn't believe me anyway. My sister Kim asked me if this was the kind of life I wanted. I said no, I didn't want to be pregnant and have a baby. A few days later, my sister Kim and her husband took me to the clinic and had them do an abortion for me. She said afterward that I was done with school, and they would take me to America, where I could begin a new life. I was very excited because we all think in Ghana that America is heaven. I began to do my housework without thinking about it.

I stopped complaining. Everything else did not matter to me at this point, but I continued to get in trouble each time my sister Lisa would come to the house. I knew I was in trouble, and each time, I wrote down how I felt. It didn't matter anymore. What I hated about housework was washing; it hurt my hands, and when we had to pound *fufu*, I hated it. I hated not being able to sit down from the time I woke up in the morning until I went to bed. It was too much, and I wasn't a fan of washing clothes.

School was approaching. I couldn't be happier to go back for my second term. Kim never took me clothes shopping; she always gave me her old clothes she didn't want, so I stole—no,

I considered that borrowing—some of her good clothes, since I didn't have any. I went to Father to get my school fees and took the bus to school. I was happy to see my friends. My old school mother Mia didn't come back, so they gave me a new school mother, the school captain, whose name was Isabella. She was so nice, lovely, and very welcoming.

I didn't have to wash my clothes because she did everything for me. This time, I was loving school even more and more. I felt free with my friends who didn't judge me. They loved me for who I was. My friendship with my best friend's brother was suddenly uncomfortable after what I had just been through.

I didn't want to be bothered; I had so much going on in my brain. I put on a brave face so my friends wouldn't ask me what was going on with me. I told my best friend's brother that I couldn't talk to him anymore. He asked me why, so I lied and told him my school mom found out and told me to end it before the other seniors found out. Also, I found out he had a girlfriend back at home, so we should stop seeing each other. After we stopped talking, he became very mean to me. I would get in trouble for no reason, but I know why, so I wasn't worried about it. I tried to do everything right. Isabella would defend me sometimes. She asked him why he was being so hard on just me, and then people began to pay attention to that, so he stopped.

One Saturday morning, I wasn't feeling too well. I told Isabella I thought something was wrong, but she looked at me and laughed and said, "Why do you always feel that way?"

I told her, "I don't know; my stomach hurts, and I feel very nervous." My heart was beating very fast, and I already knew something was going to happen. I was just not sure what that would be.

I stayed in bed all that day. My school mom was very nice; she brought lunch to me.

After a while, I heard one of my classmates running and calling my name. She came in the room and said, "You have a visitor." I looked at her and laid my head back down. She said, "Wake up; you have someone here to see you." I told her it had to be a mistake; I don't have anybody to come visit me, and I'm not that important. She said, "Get up; come on. There is a guy here to see you," so I went downstairs, and there was a guy I had never meet before. He said he was sent from the missionary house and had a letter for me.

At that point, I felt like I wanted to use the restroom, and at the same time, I felt like crying because I knew something was wrong. I didn't open the letter when he handed it over to me. I asked him what was wrong and who had died this time. He looked at me and said, "How did you know?"

I said, "I have the feeling."

He said, "Father Clement has died. He was ninety-four." I sat on the floor, speechless.

Once again, death had struck me. Again, I looked at heaven and said, "God, why? Why me? What did I do wrong?" I began to cry. No one was able to console me. As I was crying, I opened the letter. It said that he had left me money to finish the rest of the school year. He'd paid for the rest of the two school semesters that I had left.

Father was thinking about me on his death day. I felt blessed, and I felt love that he was thinking about me. He wanted to make sure I was okay before he took his last breath. Life is unfair to me. I don't understand why death seems to take away from me all the people I love and who love me.

I asked the guy what happened and whether he was sick, because I'd just seen him and he was okay. Did he get sick?

The messenger said he just went to bed and never woke up again. He stayed for a few hours to make sure I was okay. The rest of the school year wasn't fun for me anymore, but my friends and school mom cheered me on each time I got sad.

That year, we had a break when everyone got to go home for a week. It was a choice, and I was going to stay at school, but my school mom asked me to go with her, so I went home with Isabella. Her mom, dad, and sisters were very nice to me. We did a lot of fun things. That school year was her last year, so we spent much time together. I met her brother, and her mom said, "Maybe one day, you would marry my son." He was the only one who wasn't married.

I was there for one week. Every morning before they would wake up, I would sweep the whole house, take out the trash, and wash the dishes, so they loved me. When the week was over, we had to go back to school. When we were about to leave, they told me that I was welcome to come back and stay any time. I guess Isabella had told them that I lost both my mom and my dad.

We went back to school, and I was happy to see my friends. The school had a field trip, so my school mom paid for me to attend. We had a blast on the trip, and for a summer activity, I joined the school track and field team. That didn't go so well, so I joined the soccer team. That also didn't go so well, so I went back to join the hockey team. That was so much better—nobody was making fun of me.

Soon after that, the school year was over, so I went home with my school mom. A few days later, we went to a party, and I saw him. He came and talked to me. I was a very shy person during that time, but we talked for a few minutes. He asked me what my name was and how I was doing. The next week, he came to the house to visit his mom and then asked me if I would go out with him sometime. I told him that I wasn't sure, so he gave me his number to call him if I ever changed my mind.

In the meantime, I heard my sisters were looking for me because I didn't go home. They went to one of my friend's houses, so my friend told them where I was. My sisters Kim and Lisa came to my school mom's house and told them very bad things about me. They told them that I'm a thief and a liar, and that they shouldn't trust me. When my school mom and I got home, her dad called her alone. I wasn't sure what they were talking about. She came back and said that I couldn't stay with them anymore because my sisters came there and disrespected them, and she said that I should go home.

I didn't want to go home, so I begged them not make me go back there. They agreed to let me stay for a few weeks. Days later, my school mom's brother came by the house, and I agreed to go out with him. He took me to dinner, and we hung out with his friends. After that, we saw each other a few more times, and for the first time in my life, I had a real boyfriend.

One Saturday morning, I was out with James, and when I came back, they said that my third cousin also came looking for me. She also described me as if I was nothing. She told my school mom's parents to kick me out of their house because they shouldn't trust me. I hadn't seen her since dad passed, so I was surprised to see her. I believe she was doing my sisters' dirty work, so when they asked me to leave, I did. My sisters were causing too much trouble, so this time I left and went to stay at Isabella's brother James' house, where none of my relatives knew where I was. He treated me with respect.

A few days later, we were out and were standing by the side of the road when a car pulled over. It was my brother, and he said to get in the car. I said no. He asked me who I was with. I said nobody, and he said, "Why are doing this to our family? Everybody is worried about you, and we are looking for you."

I said, "Worried? Are you sure everybody was worried about me, or is everybody worried about the idea of Kim having me as a maid?"

He asked, "When you are ready, would you come home?" I said yes I would, in my own time and nobody else's.

I spent all summer break at James' house when it was time to go back to school. I had someone to drop me off at school. I didn't go by myself like I used to. It felt great. James sometimes came with his friends to visit me at school. My friends were happy to see me happy. I forgot all about my troubles, sadness, and fears. I was happy again like I used to be when Dad was alive. My friends and I would sit and talk about life. Before, I wasn't sure what mine would be like, but at last I had a boyfriend. Each time I said the word *boyfriend*, they laughed. It just felt great not to be raped, and to have someone who actually cared about me and not just the sex.

My friends Olivia, Eunice, Ava Jane, and Joyce and I would sing funny songs and dance like there's no tomorrow. I felt free and happy, I wasn't worrying about anything. The song "It Is Well with My Soul" and the song that goes, "God sent his son we called him Jesus, because he lived I can face tomorrow; all fear is gone" make me feel happy and free.

One of our roommates went home and died. It was a very sad day after we heard the news. She was fine the day before, and I felt like death was around me too much. I was not sure what to think; everybody handled the news so well. I took it harder because her bed was close to mine, so we talked every night before we fell asleep. In a few days, we all went to her funeral. She lived in a small town where they put her to rest. Every night, I looked where she always slept and felt like she was right there talking to me. Sometimes I dreamed about her, and I would wake up crying because it was too much for me. Nothing good was in my life because it was like everything I touched or set my eyes on died.

We had a few days before summer break, and the girls and boys decided to have a party for which we got in trouble. That was my first time drinking. I was drunk, and I couldn't remember where I was or what my name was. The next day, the principal punished us. We had to weed the whole school field. I'm not sure how many acres of land, but it was big enough to play soccer on it. We weeded from morning to evening, so there was no class for us. The next day, we were all going home.

James came to pick me up. I was so happy to see him. On the way home, he told me that he had to travel to America in the next two days and that I could stay at his place while he was gone. I was so sad, but he assured me that everything would be fine.

The day came, and he left. It felt like it was another death to me. I cried for days and days. He left me his cell phone, so he could call me. He called once in two weeks, but sometimes I would call, and a woman would answer the phone. Each time he called, I asked who that was, and he said that was his roommate girl. I felt something was wrong. I didn't believe him.

Two months later, the rent was due, and I couldn't get hold of him, so I had to move out. Ben, another brother, came and said that he should take over and that I should move out. I didn't have anywhere else to go. I asked him why James didn't call me. I told him if he can pay the rent himself, he can have the apartment. They were very mean, so I had nowhere else to go.

I went back to my sister Kim's house. When I got there, Kim and Lisa lectured for hours. I apologized for my bad behavior, and I promised that it would never happen again. I felt like I was back to being a maid again. I continued to do the cleaning, cooking, and washing. She had the other help, so it was not that bad anymore. My sister Kim had to travel to America, so I took care of her kids while she was away.

She was only gone for a few weeks, and I had to go back to school. That year was my senior year, and my fees were all paid by Father after his death, so I didn't I have to go back to the missionary house. I missed going there and talking to him. I went back to school, and all my friends came. We did a lot of fun things. Since it was our senior year, we sneaked out of campus and went to town at night. That night, I meet an old friend—my friend's brother, who I had had a crush on when he was a senior. We hit it off right away. We had to go back to campus before daybreak. The next morning, we started our exams for the senior final year. I studied literature, economics, and history. The test was over in two weeks, and it was time to say goodbye to this cold and beautiful place. It was a sad day for me because I might not see my friends again. We took pictures and talked all night, but when morning came, we all went to our separate places.

I went back to my sister Kim's house and continued to do what I had to do. A few months later, I started to take computer classes after my housework was done. I went to class, where I met my school mom. We hadn't spoken in a while, so we had lunch and got caught up. She said her brother asked about me all the time, but I wasn't ready to talk to him yet. One morning, our doorbell rang, and when I went to open the gate, that was when I saw this handsome guy, looking for my sister's husband. After his meeting, he left.

I said to myself, "I hope I see him again." A few days later, he came back, but only to ask me out. He didn't even finish the sentence before I said yes. He laughed and gave me his number, so I would call him when I went to class. After class, he picked me up, and we went to lunch before I went home. My sister Kim stopped questioning me, but each time Lisa would come to the house, they would go through my things.

My new boyfriend and I got serious, and I met his mom and sisters. He was the only boy, and he had two sisters. Sometimes I would go to church with them or go to their house and hang out. Within six months, we fell in love. He was the love of my life. We finally decided it was time to tell my sister, so I could introduce him to my family. The day before I told my family, he asked me to marry him.

That was the happiest day of life. I cried, but they were tears of joy. I thanked God for giving me what I had been hoping for at last—someone to love me for me. The ring was beautiful. The next day, I told my sister Kim that there was someone I wanted her to meet—Osos, my boyfriend who became my fiancé, would come over to meet her. She didn't say much, but after he left was when she began to say, "Why do you want to get married? You are so young. We were going to take you to America." She talked and talked and asked me if that's what I wanted, and I said yes, and she said okay. I was happy and in love.

Everything was okay. I began to do fewer house chores, and I was still taking my computer classes. My fiancé was paying for my classes. We went everywhere together. I was so happy, and I forgot everything I had been though almost completely, but I wasn't thinking about it constantly. I was just as happy as I could be.

After a few months, my sister Kim and her husband had a visitor from the States. He was staying with us. One day my sister and her husband called me to talk and said that this was their friend. He had a lot of money in the States and he would take very good care of me. They said this guy that I was seeing couldn't do anything for me, so I should make a choice. That news broke my heart. How could they say that?

After our conversation, I left for class. I didn't have time to call my fiancé, so I went to class. After class, I called and called him but got no answer. When I got home, Amanda said that he was at the house, talking to my sister and her husband, and at that moment, I got sick to my stomach. I knew that things would never be the same again. My life would change again for the worse.

CHAPTER 6

BETRAYAL

If have learned anything from life, it is that sometimes the darkest times can bring us to the brightest places. I have learned that the most toxic people can teach us the most important lessons and that our most painful struggles can grant us the most necessary growth. I have also learned that the most heartbreaking losses of friendship and loved ones can make room for the most wonderful people. I have learned that what seems like a curse in the moment can actually be a blessing and that what seems like the end of the road is actually just the discovery that I am traveling down a different path. I have learned that no matter how difficult things seem, there is always hope, and I have learned that no matter how powerless I feel or how horrible things seem, I can't give up hope. I have to keep going even when life is scary. Even when all my strength seems to be gone, I have to keep picking myself back up and moving forward, because whatever I am battling in the moment will pass, and I will make it through. I have made it through and will make it through whatever comes next. I told myself I could handle anything that my sisters threw at me. I kept telling myself I had been through worse than whatever was coming at me.

I asked my sister, and she said she told him the truth, which meant that she lied. That night I went to his house, and he was there. He told me that my sister and her husband said that I had demons inside me and that I was no good for him and I was a liar. He went on to say that they said I was using him and they were taking me to the States. They further told him I was going to marry their friend. He told me he needed time to process all this information that he got, so I left. I cried and cried because I thought I had found love. I kind of felt like my sister Kim was jealous of my having a young guy when she was married to someone older than her.

The next morning, I got a call from my school mom's brother James. He wanted to start things where we left off. I was unsure about it, and I told my best friend that I don't want the pain to be too much, but just in case my fiancé decided he was done, I decided to talk to James. We started talking about little things. It had been a month since my fiancé wanted a break, and I didn't have money to continue my computer classes, so I stopped and got a job four blocks away from the house. It was at a bar and grill.

After I finished the housework and the kids left for school, I would go to work. After six weeks, my fiancé reached out and said he wanted to continue the relationship. He said he would try and put everything behind him. I wasn't sure if I should be happy or not. I didn't feel excited about it, but I knew that I loved him, and that was okay with me. However, I was still talking to James. I knew he was far away, so it would not cause any harm. The only person who knew about it was my best friend.

My sister Kim and her husband were still pressuring me about her friend who came from the States. One morning, my sister and her husband went out, and her friend said to me, "You know, if you have sex with me, I will leave you alone. I would tell your sister and her husband that I'm no longer interested." So I did it, because at that point, I had nothing else to lose, and I wanted to be left alone. In a few weeks, he went back to the States. My sister and her husband never said anything to me again, so I continued my life working at the bar and talking to James.

My fiancé and I came back together, but it wasn't the same anymore. We continued where we left off. A few days later, I told him that my ring was too big, so he took it back to have it exchanged. That ring never came back, and he kept saying they were working on it. I began to have this feeling I always had when something was going wrong; I was sick to my stomach. One evening, I went to surprise my fiancé at his house, but when I got there, he was with another woman, and she had my engagement ring on! I asked him what was going on, and he said that was a friend and she was helping with the ring. I knew that was a lie. All I said was okay, but deep down my heart, I knew. I just didn't want to accept it.

We continued the relationship, and I still continued to talk to James by phone twice a week. He sometimes sent me money from the States. One day my fiancé called me at work and said I should have told him it wasn't true. I wasn't sure what he was talking about, so after work, I went to the house, where he told me that my best friend had told him that I was talking to my ex back in the States, so I lied and told him it wasn't true. Now our relationship was based on a lie. His sisters told me that he had been seeing someone, but each time I asked him, he also lied. I couldn't take it anymore. It was breaking my heart because I still loved him.

A few weeks later, my sister Kim traveled to the States. This time, she wasn't coming back. Her husband was home with the kids, so I helped him with the kids. As days and then weeks went by, everything changed. I stopped talking to my best friend because she betrayed our friendship and my trust. My fiancé and I broke up because we couldn't trust each other, and the love we had faded away.

I still loved him, but not as much. Some days I cried, not for him, but for Dad. I thought maybe if Dad were alive, things could have been different. I believe it could have been. I was helping my sister's husband take care of the kids and continued to work at the bar, where I made new friends. I started to date the owner of the bar. He had a wife, but she was outside the county. It was a new experience for me. I had never dated anyone who was married before.

One day when I got home, my fourth sister, Amelia, was there. She came with my niece, and she was coming to stay and help out. Little did I know that my life was about to change again, not for the better, but for the worse. Sometimes I felt I had been punished and God had forgotten me. Every day, I grieved for Dad. I imagined how life could have been if Dad or Mom were alive.

We were all doing okay. I would wake up, get the kids ready for school and clean the house, and then I would go to work. One day when I came home, my sister Lisa was there, and I knew I was in trouble. Each time she came around, it was because I did something. My sister Lisa and Kim's husband called me to the room and said that the phone bill had come, and it was higher than normal, so they called every number to find out who had placed those calls. Five people live in that house. My sister Lisa and Kim's husband accused me of making those calls. I told them it wasn't me, but they didn't believe me. They already had already made up their minds to kick me out of the house, so nothing I said mattered at that point.

That evening, it was raining. They said if I didn't tell them the truth, they would kick me out, but there was nothing to be told because I didn't make those calls. My sister Kim's husband went upstairs for a while to talk to Kim, I guess, and he came back down, went to my room, took all my clothes, and threw them out in the rain. He told me to get out. My sister Lisa stood there and did nothing. She told me she wished she could help, but she couldn't. I then asked her if I could stay with her for one night, but she said no. I stood in the rain while I was crying and picking my things up from the ground. I felt all alone. I felt lost. I felt I had lost all over again.

I felt defeated. I was scared and worried and not sure where I would end up. I thought I would die out there all alone. I wasn't sure what would happen to me; my worry was, where would I sleep? I didn't have anybody or any money. How would I feed myself? How could I survive out there? All kinds of thoughts were going through my mind. I felt sad, and I couldn't stop crying. I just couldn't believe what was happening. I never thought my flesh and blood could kick me out on the street when I had nowhere to go, and they were all I had.

My sister Lisa watched me cry while I picked up my things from the ground, and she did nothing to stop it or help me, so I packed all my clothes into the bag and left. I had no idea where I was going. It was raining, and I was walking in the rain, crying so hard. I missed Dad so much. I asked God to help me and show me the way, because at that point I was giving up. I had lost everything and everybody. I didn't have anybody to love me. I kept thinking about what was going to happen to me.

I got scared. What if I got raped again, or got killed? All kinds of thoughts were going through my mind. I was walking by the side of the road, and a car pulled up. I knew him because he came to the bar where I worked. He offered me a ride, but I told him I don't have anywhere to go. He said he would get me a hotel for one night so I could get out of the wet clothes. He said he would stay for a few minutes to make sure I was okay. I thought to myself, *There is something not right about this.*

I had no choice. The older guy I was dating, John, had traveled to visit his wife in the States, so we went to the hotel. He got me the room, and he left—or so I thought. When I came out from the bathroom after changing my clothes, there he was in my hotel room. I asked him how he got the key. He said he paid for it. This guy was naked.

I asked him why. He said, "Do you think I'm doing this for free?" I began to put my clothes on so I could leave, but he then grabbed me by my neck, pushed me on the bed, and punched me in my face. He started beating me as though I did something wrong. After a while, he stopped and said, "You better lie still." He then held my neck.

I couldn't breathe, and I was crying and said, "Please don't kill me. Please. You don't have to do this. Please stop. Please." He ripped off my pants and raped me while I lay there hopeless and powerless. I started crying while he raped me over and over again.

I lay there and pretended I was with Dad and we were sitting under the tree, watching the stars and singing. I could hear Dad telling me the story about how he met Mom. I couldn't remember anything else, but what I could remember was that I woke up the next day, and he was gone. I didn't know what happened after I must have passed out. I put my clothes on and ran just in case he came back. I left all my other clothes. I went to one of my friend's houses not far from work. I asked her if I could take a shower and if I could borrow some of her clothes.

I couldn't tell anybody what happened. My friend asked me what happened to my face, and I said I fell and hurt my face. I told her my sister and her husband kicked me out, and she asked me why. I couldn't speak because I was crying. I was feeling so much pain. She let me take a shower; there were many bruises on my body. I cried while in the shower and asked God why. I was eighteen years old, and the man had taken away so much from me, but I was glad he didn't kill me. When I came out from the shower, my friend asked me if I was okay and asked me why I was crying so much. I told her it was because I didn't have anywhere to go, and I missed Dad as well. She believed me, and so I went to work at the bar.

My older boyfriend was there. He asked me where I had been. He had been looking for me. I told him I thought he wasn't coming back until the next day, but he said no, he came home last night. He asked if I was okay. I said yes, but he said, "I know you; you look and sound different. There is something different about you, and what happened to your face?" I told him I fell, and I was okay and said it's just because I didn't get a good sleep, too. He gave me a look and said "hmm" the whole day.

He kept saying I looked different. I told him I had been crying because my sister and her husband kicked me out of the house, and I slept outside the gate. I knew in the back of my mind that no one would believe me if I told them I had been raped. No one had believed me before, so who would believe me now? So, I kept it to myself. It had been tough for me; I was hurting on the inside and smiling on the outside. I kept asking God, "Why me?" and wondered how long before all my suffering would end.

All day at work, I kept saying to myself to just breathe. I just need the day to be over, but as I turned around, there he was—the man who had just raped me was standing and smiling at me. He wanted his drink as usual. I was so mad and crying so hard on the inside. I served him the usual, but before I served him his drink, as he watched me and kept smiling at me, I poured his in the glass, spit in it, and handed it over to him. He then smiled, paid me, and left without touching his drink. I told him, "I hope you can sleep at night, knowing what you did to me."

He said, "I did nothing to you, and I gave you exactly what you asked for."

I said, "I did not ask you to rape me." He smiled at me and walked away.

I couldn't have been more upset. I knew it was wrong for me to do that, and I could get fired for that. I saw him talking to my boss, who was my boyfriend at the same time. I thought he was telling him what I did to his drink. After he left, my boss came over. My heart was beating so fast. He asked me if I was okay. I then breathed in and said yes. He didn't believe me. He said, "Do you want to talk about it?"

I said, "There's nothing to talk about, and I am okay."

Deep down I wasn't, and he knew I wasn't. He asked me if I wanted to stay at his guest house for now until he could find me something. I told him not today, because I wanted to stay at my friend's house for that night. I thought to myself, *I have just gone through hell; the last thing I want to do is to be with another man.* He said, "I miss you." I was quiet, and he asked me where I was going to sleep. I told him I would stay at my friend's house, and he said okay.

So, I went with my girlfriend from work; she lived in a small two-bedroom apartment with her mom, dad, and two sisters. Because of her mom and dad, I had to wait for everyone to go to sleep before coming over to the house. I would sit outside their house for hours. Work closed at 12 a.m., and I would stay up until 2 a.m. sometimes because they did family time, sitting by the fireplace and talking. When they went to bed, my friend would bring me inside the house to sleep. I had to wake up by 5 a.m., take a shower, and leave before everyone would wake up. I continued life like nothing had happened, but it was hard to forget. I buried everything inside, and that it was the only way I could live my life.

I went to work with a smile on my face. My boss-boyfriend was up early. He was there when I arrived. I smiled at him and said good morning. He shook his head and said, "I know something is wrong with you."

I said to him, "You worry too much. I'm not your wife, so stop worrying." I walked away after saying that to him, and I started to work. Every thirty minutes, he would stand in the corner and watch me. Before the end of the day, I asked my friends if I could stay with them, but she said that she wasn't going home. She was going to her boyfriend's house, so my only option was to stay with my boyfriend-boss.

I was getting ready to close when he came and said he wanted to talk to me. He said he would be at the house and wanted me to come by. I said okay, so after I closed, I went to his house. His mother was there. She didn't like me much because John already had a wife, and she didn't like the idea of him being with me. I said hi, but she didn't respond. I saw John coming down the stairs; we went up to his room. I sat on the bed, and he sat on the couch for about ten minutes. He just watched me without saying a word.

I asked him why he asked me to come over, and after ten minutes, he said he loved me and asked me to please tell him what was wrong with me. I said I was fine. He came close to me and hugged me. He touched where my bruises were, and it hurt so bad, I screamed. He asked me why I screamed, and I said my stomach hurt again. I lied to him. I was afraid that if I told him what had happened, he would look at me differently, so I would keep it to myself as long as I could. I was used to keeping things to myself.

He took me to the guest house and left. I took my shower and got dressed. I went downstairs where he was watching TV and said good night. He said okay. When I woke up the next day, he was sitting there watching me sleep. He said he loved watching me sleep. I smiled, and he didn't even try to have sex with me. I was afraid he would, but he didn't. He asked me what he could do to help. I said I need to get ready for work. To that he said, "I'm your boss; you can be late." I smiled at him and went to the bathroom to get ready.

I didn't want him to see my bruises. He asked me why I was hiding to get dressed, but I said I wasn't hiding. He said, "I know you are hiding something from me and lying about it. You have answers for every question, and you are being smart about it." He smiled at me and said, "I wasn't born yesterday, you know!" Then he left.

His house was close to the bar, so I could walk. After I got ready, I walked to work. I was not feeling okay, but there was nothing I could do, so I stayed happy on the outside and dying on the inside. I told myself nothing could last forever, and this, too, would pass. I would be whole again, and I had to stay strong and keep moving. It would be okay. That day, he didn't ask me if I was okay. I think he got it; he knew I wasn't going to tell him.

After work, I went to the guest house, and he was already there. He had brought dinner, so we ate, and afterward, I went up and took a shower. That night, he slept in the bed with me; he touched me, and I told myself that other man took sex away from me without my permission, but I could do this because John loved me, and I loved him. I pretended as if I was enjoying that sex, but I wasn't. I was hurting and crying on the inside.

This was hard, but I tried. To me, sex was nothing; it was just sex, and I didn't enjoy it. I just did it to make my boyfriend happy. Each time he touched me, I felt like it was like the man who raped me was touching me. Each time, I thought about Dad and pretended I liked it. Sometimes I would cry. It was hard, but I didn't know what to do. I didn't have a choice; I had nowhere to go, and I didn't have anybody. None of my family cared about me, so this was better.

This went on for three months. I still talked to James. I called him from time to time because I didn't have a cell phone, so he sent me money to buy a phone. I never mentioned to him what had happened to me. I only said I was staying with my friend. He said okay.

My boyfriend-boss said I should find a house, and he would rent it for me and pay for it. My friend told me not to because our boss is very controlling. He wanted to know where I was and who I was talking to, and he would get really mad if I talked to a customer for too long. He would ask me what we were talking about, and he made me cry sometimes. He would call me names—any name you could think of—and became mentally abusive. I didn't make enough money to get my own place. Back in Ghana, to rent an apartment, the landlord required a one-year deposit, and I didn't have that kind of money, so I stayed with him. My friends told me not to let him rent a place for me; if I did, my life would be over. I told them my life was already over.

I was handling the mental abuse well, I told myself. I have a thick skin, and what didn't kill me would only make me stronger. At work, he asked one of my co-workers to ask me to come and see him. No one knew about us except his mom and brother, but his behavior made it obvious, and everyone started talking about me. So, when my co-worker told me to go see him, I pretended I didn't know why. I asked her, "Why? Do you know why?" She did not know, so I went up to his office.

He asked me to sit, and he said he was sorry for his behavior and that he loved me and didn't want me to talk to people. I said, "I work for you; there is no way for me not to talk to anyone." He asked me to marry him and said that should make me happy, but I wasn't at that moment. I realized that I couldn't do that. What would other people think of me? I told him I couldn't marry him and that I was sorry. I told him I wasn't saying no because he didn't love me, but I needed someone who didn't have a wife already. He said if that's what I wanted, it was okay with him. I told him after work I would stay with my friend Amy just to clear my mind. He said okay, so I went to the guest house and got my things.

I stayed with my other friend who lived by my work. It was okay; she would be nice today, and then the next day she would be mean. I didn't know what to call that. I was never happy; I was unhappy.

Happiness was the last of my worries. None of my sisters or brothers came to look for me. One day I was off work, and when I came the next day, my co-workers told me that a man came looking for me. He said he was my sister Kim's husband, and he was asking a question about the owner of the bar. He asked them if it was true that I was dating him. They said they didn't give him any information and told him to ask me when he saw me. Life wasn't easy.

I did not even know who I was or what I was doing. I was just there. After a while, I got pregnant with John's baby, so after work that night, I told him. He told me that I couldn't have that baby because his wife was coming from out of state, and he wanted me to get rid of it. I just sat there and cried. I couldn't even speak. I went home to my friend's house and cried all night. I asked God to give me strength and asked him to guide me through this. The next two days at work, I would see him and bow down my head.

He hadn't spoken to me, and I hadn't spoken to him. Three days later, he sent me a text that said, "Tomorrow is the appointment." I said okay; when I came to work, he picked me up. He wanted to make sure it was done, so he went with me to the clinic, and I had an abortion again. He said that I should stay at the main house with him because he wanted to make sure I was okay. I heard him and his mother arguing about me. His mother told him to leave me alone and that he had a wife. I heard him tell his mother that he couldn't because he loved me. He came back to the room, but I pretended I was sleeping. The next day, he asked me if I would marry him again; he wanted me to be his second wife.

In Ghana, you can marry two, and the Muslims marry as many as four or five wives. I told him no again. I asked him, "Did you forget what you told me three days ago?" He said he was mad at me and that was why he said that. I told him I can't do this any-more. I told him I had been through so much already, and I couldn't continue to go through things with him. I said, "You love me today, but tomorrow you would say something different." I told him I couldn't be at his beck and call and that I still have power over my life and I would decide when and how I wanted to live my life. I was crying, and I told him, "You just made me have an abortion, and you are asking me to marry you. Why, when you just put my body through hell?" I was so upset that he tried to calm me down. He said okay and sorry.

He asked me what I wanted him to do to make me happy. I said nothing. I wasn't sure what I wanted. I didn't even know who I was at that time. All I knew was that I had been raped so many times, and I lost the love of my life, and my dad, and I was still grieving the loss of Dad. I'd had so many losses that sometimes I didn't even know who I was. All I knew was that I was still alive.

He started to treat me like I was his wife. I stayed with him every night. I felt safe with him, and that was what mattered to me. A few weeks later, he told me that his wife was coming back from the States, and he would let me stay at his friend's house. I told him I would rather stay with my other friend's place than at a man's house, after all I had been through. I forgot myself, and he asked, "What have you been through?" I realized what I'd just said, so I said the abortion.

After his wife came home, we hadn't spoken. He treated me like a regular employee, and on some days, he would be harsh with me. I got very sad. I was so confused. Some days, I would not eat for two days. I would cry and cry. I was in love with him, or so I thought, and he loved me—or so I thought. Maybe in my mind, it was just the idea of having someone to care for me like Dad would.

It was hard to work there, knowing that he was with someone else and not me. I missed him some days, so my friends said I needed to get another job. That was the only way I could move on from him. They told me about this boutique store where they were looking for help. They said it would help me get out of this relationship I had with a married man, so I went ahead and took the new job. I stopped working for him.

CHAPTER 7

NEW JOB, NEW FRIENDSHIP, AND FAMILY DRAMA

I didn't even give him notice, because if I did, he might have stopped me. I'm not sure at this point. After I quit working at the bar, he never called me to find out if I was okay or what happened to me. I guess he figured it out on his own, or someone told him, but I was hoping he would call me and ask how I was doing. I figure that is what all men do after they have used you, and they don't need you anymore. They throw you away like a piece of trash. In the back of my mind, I knew I never meant anything to him. Everything he said was a lie.

Dad was the only man who truly loved me. I began to hurt even more and more every day. As time passed by, I was healing, but it was hard; he was the only man besides Dad who showed me love, even if it was a lie. I felt safe with him. I was not sure how life was going to be for me without him. Some days, I missed him, so after work, I would walk by and see him talking to other women. I got very sad that he had not tried to call me or look for me.

After a month, I couldn't stay with my friend anymore. Sometimes, she would say something like "How long are you staying here?" and she would say, "You should have stayed with him. You are so stupid." It became too much for me, so I went and got a room in a big rented house; it had about fifty other women; half were my age, and half were older. We all stayed there, and it only cost $50 a month. Some of them worked during the day and some didn't, but it was better for me because we were all woman going through different things. We are all from different backgrounds. Everyone got along, and I made a few friends. I was doing okay, and in my mind, I made it feel like home. I started to smile again, little by little.

After work, I would come home early. I was scared to stay out late because my fear of being raped was at the back of my head. I didn't go out past 8 p.m., but usually, by 5:30 p.m., I was in my room or sitting outside at the gate, talking to some of the girls. I still missed John. It had been months, but I was learning to be a whole person again. I was trying to pick up the pieces of my life. I had no family, no friends, and no one to love me, but one thing that I never forgot was that God loved me. I believed that, and that was what kept me going every day.

While I was living at the hostel, my niece was living with Kim. They brought her to stay with Kim, and they kicked me out, but I'm okay with it. Sometimes I would come by Kim's house and get some food from my niece. One morning while I was at work, my friend called and said that my niece came by to her and her house looking for me, and she told her I had stolen her passport, and she wanted it back. My friend told her that I couldn't have done that and that she was holding onto my passport for me, so why would I take hers?

My friend told her where I was staying, and she went to my hostel and went through my things. She didn't find anything, and then Lisa called me and asked, "Why did you steal your niece's passport?" I told her I didn't know what she was talking about. I asked her what the name on the passport was. She said, "Why does it matter?"

I told her, "I don't even know she has one." She said I was a liar and that my niece told her that when she went to my hostel, they told her I stole some girl's diamond. I laughed and said, "Not only did you guys kick me out, but you are chasing me around town and falsely accusing me of stealing a passport and some girl's diamond. What is wrong with you people?" I said, "If you have nothing good to say, then please leave me alone." I was so shocked and hurt. I was more upset than ever, but that didn't stop my life. I continued to live day by day. Life is not easy. I realized my family really hurt me. I wondered what I had done to make my family hurt me like that. Nothing I did satisfied them, so whatever it was that I did must have been really bad. I wish I knew what I did. I could barely feed myself. Sometimes it was really hard not knowing what tomorrow might bring. I was angry at myself because I allowed myself to let people hurt me and do unforgettable things to me, and that makes me sad.

At my new job, I made a friend. His name was Jack, and he was very nice to me, kind, sweet, and very welcoming. I was scared that he also wanted to rape me like the other man, but as time went by, that wasn't the case. We became close due to the fact that his girlfriend was upset, and she didn't understand why we were so close. Nothing was going on between us; we were just friends. We understood each other. He got me; he understood me. All his friends thought there was something going on with us, but the truth is that we were just friends.

James called me one day and said I could go and stay with his mom and sister if I wanted to. I still hadn't heard back from John. I felt like everything he told me was a lie, so one day I went by and spoke to him. I asked why he never looked for me. He said that he was busy and that he was mad at me for leaving without saying anything to him. He said he thought I was done with him, so he just let it go.

I looked at him and started crying because a few months ago, he wanted to marry me. So, it was all a lie when he said he loved me and always would love me. He said things were better this way, and I should find myself a boyfriend. I was so hurt. I walked away, crying, hoping he would call for me to come back, but he didn't.

I left and went to my best friend Jack's house. His girlfriend was there, but the moment I got there and he could tell I had been crying, he asked his girlfriend if they could hang out later and said that I needed him, so she left. I cried on his shoulder for hours and fell asleep on his bed. I woke up in the middle of the night because I heard voices. It was Jack and his girlfriend having an argument because of me.

I told her I was sorry and that I would leave. I didn't want to cause any trouble between them. It was 2 a.m., and Jack said, "No, you are not leaving, and she should leave." I was shocked and at a loss for words. Nobody had ever done anything like this for me before.

She told Jack, "We are done. I hope she is wealthy." She left, and I asked him why he did that. He said I needed him the most, and that is what best friends do. He was there for me. He said, "Don't worry about her; she will come back."

The next day, I went to James' mom and sister's house, and they said I could stay there, so I went and got my stuff and came to stay with them. I hadn't spoken to any of my sisters or brothers. I was so hurt by them; no matter what, they should never have thrown me out. Family is family, no matter what. I carry that anger with me; I hated my sisters, and I never wanted to see them again.

I stayed with James' family and continued to work and hang out with Jack. James started to help me get a visa to come to the US. It was a long process. James' sister and I were very close; we went everywhere together. I went to work with her sometimes. She was more like a sister to me than a friend.

After all, she was my school mother when we were in school, so it wasn't something new. A few months after I moved in with them, the shop I worked at went out of business, so I stayed home. Sometimes I would go to work with James' sister just to get out of the house and have something to do during the day. Other days, my best friend Jack and I went shopping, had lunch, and talked for hours. He understood me; he knew me, and it felt like we had known each other our whole lives.

Whenever Jack and I hung out, I felt safe. He talked to me like Dad. I felt like he was my guardian angel. I could get mad at him for no reason, and he still stayed by my side to make sure I was okay. I knew that there was a reason for everything I had been though. God doesn't give you more than you can handle. I continued to stay in James' mom and dad's house. Every morning, I would wake up, sweep the whole house, take out the trash, and make James' mom breakfast. She was an older lady; they loved me like their own.

There was not one single day that went by that I didn't miss Dad. I missed Dad more than Mom because I was very close with Dad. I knew Dad was watching over me. James was still trying to get me to the States, but it is very difficult to get a visa to the States. We talked almost every day. I wasn't sure if that was what I wanted. I was not even sure if he was the same person I knew three years before, but at least I would have someone who loves me — or so I thought. I really didn't have much going on with me: no job and no family. Jack got hurt when I said I didn't have any family; he always said I was his family, and he wasn't going anywhere. He said he would be there whenever I needed him.

I needed something to do; I needed a job. I got frustrated and mad all the time for no reason, and I took it out on Jack. I guess I was mad about everything I had been through. I hadn't healed from it; I buried it inside me. Jack understood me somehow. I never told him that I had been raped so many times, but he got me. It was hard to explain.

I decided to go back and see if John would give me back my job at the bar. I knew it was a bad idea for me to do that, but I guess I wasn't over him, and I thought the only way to find out if I still loved him and if he still loved me was to be close to him. That was what I told myself. I didn't tell Jack because I knew he would be worried or maybe mad at me for going back to John, so one morning, I went by the bar, and he was there. I said hi, and he said he missed me. I smiled at him and asked whether I could have my job back. He said, "You are the one who left. Go to work." Just like that, he gave me back my job. But I got the job with the condition that we couldn't see each other anymore. I agreed. He asked if I had found a boyfriend yet, and I said yes. I lied. I was still talking to James, but I confused myself. John said, "Good."

I said, "You just told me that you missed me."

He smiled back at me and said, "Go to work." At the back of my mind, I still wanted him. I don't know why; maybe it was love.

My best friend Jack was mad at me when I told him. He said, "Why did you have to go back to him?" I told him I only needed a job and that I would go to work and do my job and go home at the end of my shift. Jack said that was impossible and that I couldn't do that because I still loved him. I told him that I would try, and I promised I would be okay. He looked worried.

I started working. One week went by, and it was difficult because I still loved him. I made a new friend who came to the bar every day, so we became friends. We would hang out after work, so I wouldn't think about John. One morning I asked him about his wife, and he said she went to the States. I said okay, and he smiled at me. At work, John would talk to other women and flirt with them. I was jealous. I felt like he was playing a game with me when it came to the matters of the heart. It shouldn't be like that, but with John, I guess there was nothing I could do.

One night before closing the bar, my best friend Jack came. He said he was worried about me, and he wanted to make sure I was okay. He said he would wait on me until I got off work because he knew I got scared going home in the night. I was always looking over my shoulder, so when Jack and I were leaving, John was standing there. I said goodnight to him. Jack held my hand, and we walked away together.

When I came back to work the next day, John was there. I was surprised to see him that early in the morning. He hadn't been there that early since I started working there again. My mind wasn't on anything. I said good morning, but he didn't respond. I looked at him; he seemed upset. I walked away and started doing my work. A few minutes later, he came and said, "Who was that guy?"

I said, "What guy?"

He said, "Don't act stupid, like you don't know what I was talking about."

I said, "Okay, which guy? There is no one here yet this morning."

He shook his head and said, "Who were you with last night?" I smiled at him and said it was my boyfriend. "You said to find me a boyfriend, so I did."

He said, "Don't bring him to this place again."

I said, "Sure." John was so upset at me because he thought Jack was my boyfriend. He thought I had moved on from him. It made me feel good. I felt like I got back at him for talking to all those women and making me feel vulnerable and insecure in my heart. I knew then that he still loved me, and he was just pretending; he was jealous that I was with someone else. My head felt big and bigger than myself. I thought to myself, *I got you back, asshole.*

He was watching me the whole day and hadn't left my side for one minute. It was good to feel wanted by someone who once loved you. I felt the excitement for a second, and I realized this was going to be a dangerous game, but I wanted to play it with him. If that was what it would take to get back at him, this was making me feel better. I liked the game. The next day at work, he was watching everything I did. I talked to every guy who came to the bar and smiled at everything they said, whether it was funny or not.

John got so mad at me that he came and grabbed me to the back office and started yelling and calling me names. He held on to my hand so tight that it hurt. I started crying because it hurt. I told him to let go of my hand, and he did. He asked, "Why are you flirting with every man?" and he called me a whore.

I said, "I thought you don't care and you wanted me to get a boyfriend." He looked at me and told me he never meant any of that and that he still loved me. He said his feelings for me hadn't changed, but we couldn't be together, and from that day, we should give each other respect and not do things to each other that would hurt us. I looked at him and said okay. I was hoping we would get back together, but I guess not. My heart was sad, and I said to myself that it was for the best.

At James' parents' house, his sister and I got into a big fight. I wasn't sure what we were fighting about, but I couldn't stay there. There was too much tension in the house. My new friend Alice, who I met at the bar and became friends with, and I found a place to stay with one of my friends' grandmothers. She was a very sweet older lady, who allowed us to stay there. We helped clean the house, and we stayed there for a while. When Alice would go out, I would hang out with my friend Jack.

Jack didn't like the idea that James' sister and I weren't getting along. He said I should talk with James' sister and work things out. Soon afterward, Alice moved out and left me alone, so I went and worked things out with James' sister. We worked it out, so I moved back into James' parents' house and still worked at the bar.

I'm not sure what I was doing anymore. I felt like my life was a mess; deep down in my heart, I knew it was, but I didn't know how to straighten up my life. At the bar, things became different again for me. I told my best friend Jack that I couldn't work at the bar anymore. He was happy when I said that. He looked at me with a big smile and said, "I told you from the beginning, but you are stubborn; you don't listen to anything."

After a few months, I got an interview at the American embassy. Jack was so happy. He went with me. I got the visa. I couldn't believe it. From the embassy, we went to buy my ticket. I couldn't wait, but at the back of my head, the unknown was killing me. What if James wasn't who he was years ago?

Jack said, "You are going to America, but if it doesn't work out, you can do anything you set your mind on. I asked Jack to promise me that we would still be friends and stay in touch with each other, and I asked him to promise me he was still going to be there for me. I started crying. Jack said nothing would change and he would be here and he wouldn't go anywhere. He would be with me wherever I was.

The next day, I went to work at the bar for my last day working there. When I got to work, John was there. I told him that day would be my last day working. He said okay, so after work was over, I said my goodbye. He didn't ask me any questions; he did not ask me why I was leaving. I guess that was the best and easiest way out for John and me.

CHAPTER 8

MOVING TO THE UNITED STATES

The day I got my visa to United States of America was the happiest day of my life. I was so excited I couldn't sleep that night. I couldn't wait for this new chapter of my life. I was wondering how I would feel once I got to the States. So many things were going on in my mind, but mostly I felt happy. Whatever that place was like, it would not be too bad. People said it was the second heaven, so I couldn't wait to be there. I don't remember if I told God thank you.

I went home for a few days before leaving for the States. I went to see my sister Lisa, and I told her I was leaving for the States. She didn't believe me and said, "Before you go, could you bring me your purses because you could buy better ones in the States?" I looked at her and thought, *Wow, I don't even know why I went there.* Maybe I thought she would apologize to me for not having my back and not being there for me, but I was wrong. I didn't get any of those. The next day, I called my sister Kim in the States, and I told her that I was also coming to the States. She sounded like she was happy for me, but she wasn't.

A few days later, I went to Dad's house in the small town just to visit, and when I got there, I felt his presence. I went to where Dad was lying on the day he died, and I cried and cried and cried. The room became so cold, and I felt a hand on my shoulder. I looked around, but no one was there. I began to leave. I heard a voice call my name. I turned around; no one was there. I was scared to death. It was my Dad. I should not have been scared, but the truth is, I was. I talked with one of my uncles, who said that the reason why I could still hear Dad or see him was because he had something to tell me. He said maybe Dad had unfinished business, and he would try other ways to communicate with me.

He said Dad never got the choice to do that, so he had been trying to find a way to tell me. That scared me. I didn't know I how I would feel if I saw Dad again face-to-face, knowing that he had died. So many things were going through my mind, including fear. I didn't know, so I asked my uncle how this could stop, and he said, "Your dad loves you, and he would never hurt you, so don't be afraid." I looked at my uncle and said, "I don't know if I can, but whatever happens, I'm sure I will be fine." I went back to the city that same day. I wasn't sure why I went to Dad's hometown; maybe I was hoping he would be there. Part of me still couldn't believe he was gone.

Shortly after my visit to Dad's hometown, my second uncle also passed away. I wasn't sure what to make of it. He was just fine right before he passed. My third uncle was sick, and I knew I couldn't go to the funeral. I was getting ready to come to America. My third cousin called to tell me. I told her I would try, but I didn't go; a few days after the funeral for my second uncle, I got a call saying that my third uncle had also passed away. I was speechless.

I couldn't believe it. I was leaving the next day, so I didn't go to this funeral either, but it hurt to lose every family member I had ever known. However, none of them was there after Dad passed away. They took over Dad's business and left me to rot in hell. Even then, I wasn't mad at them, but maybe God has a way of punishing people, or maybe Dad's ghost punished them all for not caring for me. I tried not to think too hard or beat myself up about it. After all, in life, things happen, I told myself.

My best friend Jack and James' sister took me to the airport. It was a twelve-hour flight. I slept for most of it. The plane landed at the New York City airport. I went through customs, and when I got outside, James and his friends were there. They picked me up. We went to a birthday party before going home. James lived in New Jersey, and his friend lived in New York. James had a roommate; they have been friends since they were little kids. The second day I was in America, James was off work, so he took me to a mall, and we did a little shopping. I was so happy. Everything was different from back home: the food was different, and the people looked nice.

I had a McDonald's meal for the first time. It was different from the food back home. I loved the food and couldn't get enough of it. I felt like I was in heaven; I was happy. Being with James didn't feel weird; it felt natural.

I would go for a walk in the neighborhood just to look at the people and the beautiful houses. I couldn't believe I was here in the United States. For a second, I forgot my troubles. I would take the bus, go to the mall, and just walk around, looking at the beautiful clothes. The shops at the mall had so many beautiful things. I said to myself, *When I get a job, I'm going to buy all these things*.

I would stand outside and breathe in the air. It felt good. I felt happy, but sometimes when James would go to work, I stayed home alone. I didn't have any friends yet, so I would go online and chat with my best friend Jack. I missed him. We would talk for hours and hours. I never told James about my friend Jack. I didn't think it was necessary for me to tell him since Jack and I were only friends.

I didn't think it was a big deal that each time James left the house, I would talk with Jack. One day I left my chat window open, and James went on my chat, pretending to be me and telling Jack that I missed him and how much I loved him, which was confusing for Jack. Jack thought he was talking to me, so he said he asked what I was talking about. He said we were just friends, and he asked if I was feeling okay and if I hit my head hard. The next day, I went online, and Jack asked me how I was doing and asked what that was about yesterday. I didn't understand what he was talking about, so he video-called me, and he told me he was confused about my behavior yesterday.

I asked him what he was talking about, so he told me. I told him it wasn't me. I wasn't even at the house. He said to check my chat page, but it had been cleared. I answered, "Maybe it was James; he thinks you are my boyfriend. I didn't ask him." I just left it alone. I went to the mall to find a job, and on my way back, I took the bus. I got lost; I had taken the wrong bus. My phone battery was dying, and I had to call James before my battery died. I was able to tell him where I was. James doesn't drive either, so one of his friends would come to pick me up. I was scared. Every thought in my head was, *What if I get raped here, too, and what if they kill me afterward?* I was standing on the side of the road. I wasn't sure how long before they would get there. My phone was dead. They arrived after a while.

They both laughed at me and said, "Welcome to America." I told them I was scared. James and his friend said nothing would happen to me. The next morning, his friend from New York came to visit, and so I met his wife and kids. I became friends with her. She would call me and ask me how I was doing and how things were. She was very nice and very welcoming

Winter came. It was my first time seeing something like this. The snow was beautiful and so cold. I walked in the snow and took pictures. I liked being in America. When James would go to work, I would sit home think about Dad and how much I missed him, but I knew that with God, all things are possible. I knew He had a better plan for my life, and that was why all the bad things happened to me. I began to understand a little bit, but with time, I would understand even better.

I was hoping I would get my first job at the mall after months in America. However, the day I was supposed to start work, I got really sick; I couldn't eat or keep anything down. James took me to the hospital, where they said I was pregnant. That was when everything began to change again. James had completely changed; he was so mad. He said he didn't want a baby and that he wasn't ready for one.

He then told his friend in New York that I had trapped him. I don't even know what that meant. We didn't get along, but I guess he was trying. I told him that I was not having another abortion. Before James left for the States, I was pregnant by him, and he made me have an abortion. I told him that I was tired. He was very upset at me.

Anything I would eat came right out. Sometimes when his roommate would cook, I would hide in the closet because the smell of the food made me nauseous. I would hide for hours at a time. James' roommate had a girlfriend from Kenya in east Africa. She was very nice she taught me a few things and how they were pronounced here in the US. James friend's Luck and his wife Evelyn from New York came to pick me up, and I stayed with them for two months.

She took very good care of me and helped me through my pregnancy. She was nice and tried to make me laugh even when I didn't feel like it. She cooked for me, and I never had to do anything. We become good friends. She is very funny. She has two beautiful kids who are twins: a boy and a girl. They are so beautiful and very respectful. She encouraged me to put everything in God's hands. She was an amazing person.

After a while, James came to pick me, but when we got back to New Jersey, I still couldn't keep anything down, so I ended up in a hospital for two days. We came home after two days of being at the emergency room. I was feeling a lot better. Things between James and me were very strange, but I guess we were both coping with it. After all he spent to get me to America, he wouldn't have done that if he didn't love me. We learned to get along. It wasn't great, but at least I had a place to sleep. Sex wasn't taken from me. I did it by choice, even though I didn't feel like it.

I was compromising with James, and we were working on things. He had accepted the fact that I would be keeping the baby. Sometimes we would go for a walk and just talk, and I felt like things were getting better. When I was four months along in pregnancy, James and his roommate were not getting along. He decided that we should move to Lexington, Kentucky, so we packed up and moved. We got a two-bedroom apartment. Soon after we moved, James got a job. I stayed home because I still couldn't keep anything down. James had friends there, and some of them were married, so I got to be friends with a few of them.

I found a doctor's office. I would take the bus every time I went by myself. James had never been to a single doctor's appointment with me. I did everything alone. I felt like I was in this alone. We slept in separate bedrooms as if we were roommates. I think it was better that way.

Some days I would cry. I still didn't understand why a man could not love me fully. I felt like there was something wrong with me. I would talk to myself and say, "Maybe someday, everything will make perfect sense, and so for now I will laugh at confusing things." I smiled though the tears and kept reminding myself that everything happens for a reason. I had been though a tremendous amount of pain and change in my life for the last few years, but there was still part of me that wasn't ready to give up. I would still keep on fighting a good fight.

I knew God was on my side, and I knew Dad was with me. I never understood why we couldn't get past the people we loved and lost. We still held on somehow, and every day I reminded myself that even though Dad was gone, he was still with me because sometimes I felt someone was watching me or following me. I know it was Dad.

I miss Jack so much. He was the only one who understood me, and he never judged me, no matter what. He made me laugh, and for a second, I forgot my troubles. Jack was a brother I never had.

He was my best friend, my everything. He knew what to say to make me feel better.

The baby inside gave me hope. I would talk to myself, thinking it was a girl. I always wanted a baby girl. When I had my ultrasound, the doctor said that it was a boy. It was weird; I was a little disappointed because I wanted to have a little girl, but I think Dad came back as my son. That was my thinking, but God had a different plan. As long as he was healthy, that was all that mattered. I was too big. Most people thought I was having twins. I gained a lot of weight after I could eat okay after six months. When I was bored, I ate and ate.

The doctors said that I was getting too big, and I needed to exercise, so some days I would go for a walk. James began to come around little by little. Sometimes, we didn't talk to each other for two days at a time. I was fine. I didn't care anymore; after all, I had been by myself all my life, and I expected it. In the meantime, I hadn't spoken with Jack for a while and missed him a lot. A lot had happened, and I needed to tell him. He was the only one who understood me, so I called him. He was so happy to hear my voice, and I was so happy to hear his, as well. We talked for hours.

I told him everything that had been going on, and he said it would be okay; I should just believe in God, and He would make all things possible. I was so happy to speak with him. I told him I wished he was here with me. When I was around Jack, I felt safe. He was my safe haven. I could say and do anything without worrying he would judge me. He was my brother from another mother. I loved him; he got me when no one else did. He believed in me when none of my family did. We talked and talked and laughed. It felt good to laugh. After a while, we said our goodbyes.

James told his friends that I came to this country with a different mindset. He wanted me to be a housewife or a girlfriend who went to work and came home to cook, clean, take care of the baby, and do the laundry and put it away. Back home in Ghana, the woman was supposed to do the cooking and the cleaning and washing clothes, but when I got here, things were different. James wanted a woman who didn't speak up for herself, and he hated me for that.

At the beginning, he treated me like I was his one and only. He was an amazing person who I believed loved me, and all his family loved me. However, once the baby was involved, everything changed. He made me feel like I was nothing, and it hurt so much. I felt like he was treating me like my family treated me. That brought back painful memories, but I had to keep breathing and remembering that no situation is permanent and that God doesn't give you more than you can handle. My body was built for that, and I could handle anything. That was what I kept telling myself.

Meanwhile, I had spoken with my sister Kim a few times when I came to the States, so when we moved to Kentucky, James and I went to visit her. She gave me a lot of baby clothes, a car seat, and a baby crib. It was Thanksgiving Day, and my niece was there. Kim brought her to the States instead of me. I wasn't mad at all. I was happy for her. I was also here, so it worked out for the best. It was nice to see my sister Kim again.

This time, I wasn't her maid; I was just her sister. I never forgot the things I did, and the things she and Lisa and her husband did to me, but I had grown a lot, and I learned how to let go. At least, I was trying to do that. We had a nice Thanksgiving dinner, and then we went back to Kentucky.

Things seemed to be getting a little bit better with James. I think he had accepted the fact that this baby was not going anywhere, and we began to enjoy each other's company. We tolerated each other. I was going to make it work for the baby's sake, and the fact that he spent all this money to bring me to the States and the love I had for him. I loved him, but I wasn't *in love* with him because so much had happened over the years, and it had changed things and it had changed me. James sometimes took me to the mall for a walk. We sometimes went to the park, which felt normal.

The baby would soon be here, and I was so excited. I couldn't wait to meet him. My life with James wasn't interesting; we had nothing in common. However, I was very loyal, a woman of my words, and I was willing to make it work with him no matter what; my loyalty laid with him.

Chapter 9

Baby on Board

My pregnancy wasn't easy. It was a tough journey, but when the baby moved and kicked, it was an amazing feeling. I couldn't wait to meet him. I talked to him and sang for him; it felt great.

The baby was two weeks overdue, so when I went to the hospital, the doctors admitted me. After hours in the hospital, I wasn't having any contractions, so the doctors induced my labor. After that, I started having contractions, but they were not strong enough for the baby to come out. After being in labor for forty-eight hours, I was so hungry and in pain. The doctors would not allow me to eat; they kept giving me ice chips, but it didn't help. After a while, the baby wasn't breathing, so they put oxygen on me. After a few hours, they had to do an emergency C-section. I was scared because I didn't want anything to happen to my baby.

The doctor said everything would be okay and that I should come down. They took me to an operating room. James was by my side; it felt good having him there to hold my hand. After a few minutes, there he was—I had a beautiful baby boy who weighed eight pounds and two ounces. That was the happiest day of my life. When he came out, I couldn't stop looking at him. He looked a little like my dad, or maybe me. I was not sure, but it was a good thing that he looked nothing like James.

James named him Matthew. I wasn't sure what the meaning was, so I looked it up. Matthew came from the Greek transliteration of the Hebrew name meaning gift of Yahweh. He was also called Levi and was one of the twelve apostles. He was a tax collector and supposedly the author of the first gospel in the New Testament. I kept the name because I liked it.

We stayed at the hospital for two days, and we were discharged on the third day. James was working, so his friend's wife came to pick us up. We got home, and I didn't have anyone to show me how to take care of a new baby, but I had helped my sister Kim back home when she had her baby, so that helped a little. I was being careful not to hurt him with his belly button and everything. I called my sister Kim and told her I had a baby boy. She said she would come visit and also spoke with my other sister Amelia in Chicago and told her, but none of them came to visit. I was doing everything on my own. We lived on the second floor, and because I had had a C-section, the doctor said not to do any heavy lifting.

I thought the baby would bring us closer, and things between would change, but nothing changed. I felt alone like it had been all these years, but I had my son, and that was joy.

After two weeks, I had to take Matthew for checkup. James was at work, so we took the bus. I had to lift him with the car seat, which was very hard because I was still in pain from my C-section. When we got to the bus stop, some people helped me with him. I went to every doctor's appointment by myself. I was still at home, not working. After a few weeks, I decided to go visit my sister Kim in Ohio, so James bought me and Matthew a ticket to go visit Kim.

Kim and her friend came to pick us up at the Greyhound station. Kim looked happy to see us, and we spent a week with her. It was great; it felt like when I first went to her after Dad passed. It felt like old times, and after a week, we went back to Kentucky.

I would cook, clean, and do laundry. After Matthew was six months old, I got a job at the supermarket. The pay wasn't much, and one lady at our apartment complex babysat Matthew. She charged me $10 a day, and I worked twenty-five hours a week. The pay wasn't much, so when I got paid, I would pay the babysitter and buy Matthew's food and diapers and food for the house. I had no idea that James was mad at me. The next morning, we had a big disagreement. He said each time he got his paycheck, he kept it in the drawer for me to see, but I hid my paycheck. He went on saying he paid all the bills in the house, which I already knew. I couldn't understand why he would get upset. He thought I was hiding my money, but that wasn't the case. I explained what I was doing with the money to him, but James would be James.

Some days, when I missed the bus to work, I would walk from our apartment to my work, which was about fifteen miles away. I made a friend at work, whose name was Amy. Amy would sometimes give me a ride home. Some mornings, when I worked weekends, James would drop me off. He had a car then, but he got really mad when I ate in the car. He loved that stupid car more than himself. He would not allow me to bring my drink into the car, and sometimes I had to finish the drink before getting in the car. I said it was just tea, but he still would not allow me to bring it inside the car. Sometimes he would forget to pick me up, so I would walk home.

I lost a lot of weight because I wasn't happy. When James was home and I was cooking, he would not pick Matthew up when he was crying. I would hold Matthew in one hand and use the other hand to cook. James' friends would bring me their kids to babysit, and they would go out and not come back until morning like it was okay. One day, James was going to the car wash, and I asked him to take Matthew with him, but he refused. I began to notice he didn't like his own son because he didn't want to hold him. He didn't care for his son or me. I understood he didn't want me to have him when we both find out I was pregnant with Matthew, so it all made perfect sense. I wasn't surprised, but I thought that things would change once the baby was born.

After a while, I got another job at a clothing store, and they paid me more, but things between James and I weren't good. He didn't care what I did, and we hardly talked to each other. I was trying to make sense out of my life and to understand, but he didn't give me much respect. He didn't treat me like I was the mother of his son. James didn't even care about his own son at all—he never wanted him from the beginning. When I went to work, I felt happy, but I was afraid to come home because I wasn't happy there. I was sad all the time. I didn't have a lot of friends, so I kept a lot things to myself. My friend Evelyn lived in New York, and we talked a lot on the phone when I was home, and sometimes I talked with my other sister, Amelia.

One afternoon, my friend Evelyn called me and said James called her and told her about all the conversations that we had. She said James said he had been recording my phone calls. He then went to that extent and called my sister Amelia and told her same thing. James called every person I spoke with and told them that he'd heard our conversations. Every day when I got off work, I didn't feel like going home. I was unhappy and felt like I was walking on eggshells each day. James didn't care about Matthew, as if he wasn't his own.

With time, things got a little better, and I got pregnant again. James said he wasn't ready for another baby. I told him I wasn't going to have an abortion. He would not talk to me for days until I gave up and said okay. He sent me to the clinic both times I was pregnant. We both went to the clinic. I told myself I couldn't do this anymore after the two abortions.

Things went from bad to worse, and I decided to visit my sister Amelia and her husband in Chicago. They received us with open arms. They picked us up from the bus station, and we went home. My sister Amelia and her husband were so nice to Mathew and me. He is such a good husband to my sister. I saw the way he treated my sister. She was happy. Her husband treated Matthew like he was his own son. Matthew was so happy. I'd never seen my son this happy. I was glad we came to visit them. My sister and her husband took care of us, and we stayed for two weeks.

We went back to Kentucky, but things were not the same with James. We endured a lot of heartache. I didn't understand why I was still with him. Sometimes, he would go out and come back the next day without telling me where he was. It came to a time when I didn't care to ask because he didn't care about Matthew and me. Things were not getting better; life wasn't getting any better, but I hoped that someday it would get better. I decided to go back and visit my sister Amelia and her husband again. They welcomed Mathew and me nicely like the last time. Before, we had never been close after everything I had been though and how my family had rejected me as a sister.

I have forgiven her; after all, she is my blood sister, and I'm building a relationship with her. Her husband bought me a bus ticket, so I told James that we were going back to visit my sister Amelia again, but he didn't say a word. A few days later, we left for Chicago; it was almost Christmas.

When we got there, my sister and her husband picked us up from the bus station. I was so happy to get away from James. The next day, my sister and her husband took Matthew and I to town. It was nice, and Matthew was so happy.

On New Year's Eve, Amelia went to church. I didn't go with her because Matthew was sleeping. Her husband stayed home as well. We were watching the ball drop on TV, and we were talking. I was telling him about my issues with James. I began to feel like I could trust someone besides my best friend, Jack. However, in less than a minute, everything changed.

It was midnight. The ball dropped, and he said Happy New Year to me and then asked if he could hug me. He hugged me too tight, and I asked him to let me go, which he did. He then knelt before me and said, "I want you."

I said, "I don't understand."

He said, "Can James make love to you?" I asked him why. He said, "I would make love to you very well." I felt very uncomfortable and told him to get up, and he did. I told him I'd just started building a relationship with my sister and I didn't want anything to come between us. I also told him that I didn't know how I could live with myself knowing I had slept with my sister's husband. She was the only sister I was getting close to, and I would like to continue that relationship with her.

He said she would never know because he was not going to tell her and that he could come to Kentucky from time to time and stay in a hotel so he could see me. I felt sick to my stomach. I didn't understand why my whole life revolved around someone I knew who would try and take sex away from me and was never giving me a choice. I was trying to make sense out of it, but I couldn't. I told him I could never do that. I wouldn't be the one to break my sister's heart or break up her marriage, and I would not be the one who came between them. I couldn't live with myself if I'd done that. I told him that I respected him so much and looked up to him. He said he was sorry to even try something like that, and he said we should forget it and pretend it never happened. I said okay, but deep down in my heart, I knew I couldn't forget about it, and I couldn't tell my sister, either, because she would never believe me, so I kept it with me. It was killing me not to be able to tell anyone.

I was so uncomfortable. Not long afterward, my sister came home, and we went to bed. The next day, I didn't allow my sister to leave us alone in the house with him. We went everywhere with her, even if I didn't feel like going. After two days, we left to go back to Lexington. I felt like I couldn't take a break from all this.

James wasn't too happy to see us. I felt things with him were not getting better and, in fact, were getting worse every day. A few days later, when we got back to Kentucky, my sister's husband started calling almost every day. One morning, James went to work, and I was home with Matthew when he called and asked if I had a minute to talk. I said yes. He went on and on about how he felt about me and how much he loved me. He said he wanted to go out with me and take good care of me and my son. I asked him why he wanted to do this behind my sister's back. He said it was because

82

he had feelings for me. I got so confused when he told me to think about it, and he would call me.

After I got off the phone, I felt sick. I felt like it was a dream—maybe I *was* having a bad dream, and I was trying to wake up from it. I didn't understand why my whole life was like that, with men trying to take something from me. A few days later, he called again. I didn't want to answer the phone, but he kept calling, so I took the call, but I told him I loved my sister, and for the first time in my life, I felt like I was in a good place with one of my sisters. She trusted me, and I didn't want anything to disrupt the relationship I had with her. If he kept pushing me, I would never respect him, and he would become my enemy. I told him if something happened between us, I didn't know if I would be able to live with myself for the rest of my life. I asked him if he thought he would be able to keep this thing that he was trying to do with me a secret. He might be able to get away with it today, but tomorrow he couldn't, and when the secret came out, my family would hurt me.

I told him he couldn't use me to break up his marriage. I would not and could not be the reason his marriage would be over. I love my son, and for the first time in my life, I had someone who loved me, and he was my life. I wanted to be happy, and I wanted my son to be happy. After all the talk, he said he respected my decision and told me I'm a good person with a good heart and that I should never change for anyone. After I hung up the phone, I was in a shock. I was shaking. I didn't know who to tell this this to. It was weighing heavily on me. I was not sure what to do with this information I had.

I had a lot of things going through my mind. I knew life was about choices, so how I lived it was up to me. I was no longer ten years old. I began to ask myself why life had to be this way. Life is so unfair. I asked myself why for hours, but no one could answer that for me but me. However, I would not give up; there is always hope. With God, anything is possible. The love I had for my son kept me going every day.

When James was home, he was either on the phone or on the computer the whole time, or one of his friends came over to the house or he took his car to the car wash. He never had time to play with his own son. I felt like he didn't want Matthew. I believe he didn't because he never wanted me to give birth to our son. He didn't care for me or our child. Sometimes I would cry myself to sleep and ask myself what I was doing. He said he loved me, but he made me cry all the time. I missed my best friend Jack. It had been a while since we spoke, and I had so much to tell him.

I felt unhappy with James. I didn't feel like I was at home because he was always recording my calls. I didn't know how he did it, but he did. I kept telling myself I couldn't do it anymore. I needed to take Matthew and move away from there. This life was not about me anymore because I had a son, and I had to make a better life for him and me. I didn't have any more love in me to give James; we hadn't been sleeping in the same bed for three months, and I thought he was seeing someone else. How much more does a girl have to take?

I felt like a fool. One of my friends told me, "If you feel too used and you feel you have nothing else left inside, you should ask yourself, 'What do I have to give my son and myself?'" Sometimes things didn't go the way I wanted them to, but as years went by, it got better. At that moment, the man I was with made me feel like nobody, and it hurt so badly. I had so much pain in my heart. I had been hurt so many times in this life, and I didn't know why, and I kept asking myself why, but there was no answer to that.

Each time I cried, I could see the look on his face, like he was happy to see me cry and to see me in pain. It broke my heart and hurt so badly. Even with the way things were going on between me and James, deep down, I wanted to stay with him and make things work. I knew he had done so much for me, and I wanted to stay because of that, but I was hurting more every day. Therefore, I decided to move to Ohio. I told him that I needed a break from us, and I went to go and visit my sister Kim for a little while. He said okay, so on April 15, 2005, I packed all my stuff, and James drove Matthew and me to Ohio.

I didn't have a car in Ohio, and they only have buses in a few places. My other sister Amelia gave me some money, and Kim's husband said that he had a car he could sell to me for $1,500. That was how much I had. James taught me how to drive just a little bit, so when we arrived at Kim's house, she seemed happy. I knew her behavior, but I thought that after all these years, she could have changed. That is what I thought at the back of my head; I kept thinking that way, but who knows?

Upon my arrival, Kim's husband asked for the money, so I gave it to him, and he showed me the car. James and I both took it for a test drive, and he later went back to Kentucky. The next day, I realized the car didn't have a radio in it, but I didn't care. As long as it was drivable, it was okay with me. My sister Kim's intentions weren't good; later on, Kim introduced me to her friend. He was a very nice man who told me if I ever needed anything, I should let him know. I thought to myself, *I have been here before; the last time a man said this to me, I got raped.* This time was different because I was a little older, and I knew better, so I would not let this happen again.

My niece was still staying with my sister. A few days later, I began to look for a job. My niece worked the night shift, and she said I could leave Matthew with her, but each time I left Matthew with my niece, my sister Kim would call me and ask me where I was, saying, "You keep leaving Matthew with Ann. I didn't bring her to America for you to leave your kid with her."

Sometimes when I was going to look for a job, I would take Matthew with me. He was only two years old, and I would ask myself which company would hire someone who came to file an application with their kid. Kim's friend would help me find a job, so one morning I went to his mechanic's shop, and he took both Matthew and me to the temp agency. He and Matthew stayed in the car while I filled the application out.

Afterward, he took me to his friend's house and spoke with her to babysit Matthew.

I got my first job with the temp agency. A few days later, the temp agency called me and gave me a job at a warehouse. My first day of work started at 7 a.m. I left my sister's house at 6 a.m. to drop off my son off before going to work, but I got lost on my way to the babysitter's house.

With all my sisters, I felt like I was constantly walking on eggshells: they were so judgmental, and they didn't trust me. They always thought the worst of me, but no matter what they did to me, I still loved them. I didn't think they felt the same way about me. The love that mattered to me most was the love of God. Sometimes I lost faith, and it was hard for me to get it back. I didn't pray to

God like I should have, but I was holding on to hope, and that was what was helping me through everything. I never gave up on hope.

Hope is a powerful thing. We don't see it, but it works. I hoped that God still loved me with all my flaws. My best friend Jack was an amazing person, who was always there for me. I could not trust anybody but him; every other friend I made took from me and left and caused me more pain. I stopped making friends with women because they always betrayed my trust and hurt me.

The only friends I had were my son and my friend Evelyn. I didn't trust my sisters, but I gave them the benefit of the doubt. I kept saying to myself that this time, it would be different, but deep down, I knew I was lying to myself. When I first came to America, I called my sister Kim to let her know. I thought she would be happy, and she sounded happy on the phone and said welcome. However, a few months later, my niece said that Kim called me stupid and said, "Look at her; she also came to America. Who does she think she is?" It hurt me that my own sister made me feel like I was nobody.

I knew she never liked me, which brought up the question I kept asking myself: Why did she not like me? I knew they were just my sisters, but we were still family. We had different dads, but we were still family. Maybe if Mom had been alive, things could have been different.

I have a sister from my dad's side I never met, but I heard about she lived in the Ivory Coast. One summer when school was out, I traveled to the Ivory Coast. I was not sure what to expect from her, since we had never met before. I went with a friend who knew her. My first time meeting her, she welcomed me with open arms. She accepted me and showed me love like nobody had ever showed me. It felt good. She was married with three kids, and she didn't have enough money, but it wasn't about the money. It was how she accepted me. I stayed with them for two months. It was different. The food was nice. She would sit up with me all night and talk with me about how Dad did not accept her because she chose to live in the Ivory Coast. Dad thought she was into prostitution because almost all people who traveled there became prostitutes. Dad didn't talk to her because he thought that way about her, but the truth was, she was married and happy.

After staying there for a few months, she told me that if I had come five months before, she could have bought me so many things. She said they had been robbed few months before, and they stole everything they owned. She sold some of her clothes to buy me a ticket back home to Ghana, and she gave me money even though she didn't have any. I was very grateful for that because back in those days, we didn't have access to a phone. I lost contact with her for years.

I often thought about her and her beautiful family. I hoped to find her one day. After years of not knowing how to contact her, she called me and said someone told her where I was and gave her my number. I didn't care who did it, but I was glad I could find her. She had moved back to Ghana. I wanted to help her. I didn't have much, but I tried to give what little I could. I would buy food and drinks and ship it to her. She lost one of her daughters in a car accident, and she had health problems, so I would buy meds and ship them with the food.

She wanted to start a small business, so I sent her money to start that business. Every six months, she would call and complain about how things were not going on well, and each time I asked her what had happened to the money I gave her for the business she wanted to start. She would say it was not going well. I gave her more money. I told her I don't have money, but I was trying to return a favor because of what she did for me years ago. I was realized she was using me, taking advantage of me by asking for money all the time. I stopped giving her money because I didn't have any. I tried to send them food instead of sending her money. I would send them two bags of rice, cooking oil, and canned food. She still asked me for money, so each time she asked me about money, I told her how things had been bad for me, and that was the truth.

CHAPTER 10

TRY TO MAKE IT

My sister Kim's friend Joe told me that since I couldn't find the babysitter's house and I was running late for my first day at work, I should drop Matthew off at his shop, and he would babysit him for me until I got off work. Matthew was two years old. I dropped Matthew and left for work at my new job. You would be lucky to get work; they picked who worked and who went home. I was picked. I needed this job, so when they picked me, I worked very hard to make sure they picked me every time. At lunch, I would sit in my car; my car didn't have a radio, so I would sit and just think about how far I had come, and I tried to figure out life and wished Dad was alive.

After work was over, I went to Joe's shop to pick up my son. Joe was really nice to me and Matthew. He then made me drive, and I followed him to the babysitter's house, and I was able to find my way home. When I got home, my sister Kim started asking why I left my son at the mechanic shop filled with dirt. She went on and on for thirty minutes. I just stood there and watched her talk and talk. I couldn't say anything back because I respected her no matter what, and I didn't want to disrespect her for any reason.

The next morning, I woke up early and dropped Matthew off at the babysitter and left for work. Work lasted from 7 a.m. to 3 p.m. After work, it was raining heavily. I picked Matthew up, but on the way, I couldn't see anything because the windshield wiper didn't work. I had to pull over at the side of the road until the rain stopped. I couldn't believe my sister allowed her husband to sell me a car for $1,500 that had no radio and no windshield wipers, knowing I had a kid who was going to be in the car with me. Once I was at a light, and the car turned off on its own, and I had to restart it. I could have been on the highway, and the car might have just stopped.

I'd forgotten that my sister never cared about me. I don't know what made me think things would be different then. After the rain stopped, we went home. Each time I would go out, my sister Kim would call me and ask me where I was and what I was doing. If she didn't call me, she would make my other sister Amelia call and yell at me or talk to me I like I was still a kid.

One evening when I got home from work, my sister Kim said that her husband wanted me to pay $200 a month for rent. I told her I didn't make much. My pay rate was $8.00 per hour, and I didn't get work every day. She said I could either pay rent or move out. She told me she was about to travel to Ghana in about a month. I asked if I could help out with food instead, so I could save my money to move out. She said they didn't need food, but they wanted $200 a month. I said okay. She said my niece was paying $400, and she was taking care of her kids, so they couldn't allow me to not pay anything.

The next day, I went to see Joe, and I told him what my sister had said. Joe was upset. He asked me why my sister was doing that and asked if she forgot that I had a kid with me. After I left, I think Joe called them and spoke to them. On my way home, I felt like I was in trouble. When I got home, it was World War III. My sister went on and on about how ungrateful and unappreciative I was and how she was trying to help me. She was upset that I was going around, telling people her business. I told her I was sorry. I went in my room and cried. I felt like history was repeating itself.

I spoke with my friend Evelyn, who said I should look for a place, and she would help me. I could pay her back whenever, and she hated to see me cry. I could never leave Matthew at home with my niece without Kim being upset at me. Kim said she didn't bring my niece to America to babysit my son and that she brought her to help her with her kids, not mine. I had to take my son with me, even if I was going to fill out an application for a job. I asked myself who would give me a job when I had to bring my son to fill out a job application.

Each time I would go out, Kim would call Amelia and tell her I was out driving around and wasting gas. I asked myself what her problem was because she wasn't the one buying gas for my car. I know Kim didn't like me and that she hated me for whatever reason. She was the only one who knew why.

Kim and her husband told me to send my son to Ghana so I could work and save money, but I told them no. James also asked to send our son away to Ghana. I told them I wanted to have my son with me so he could grow with me and get to know me, and I could get to know him. They were upset, but I didn't care. I was going to do my best to take care of my son.

Things were hard. James didn't call us much or send money for Matthew. My job would pick me today, and tomorrow they wouldn't, so when I went to work, I worked harder than the rest of the people so they would pick me the next day. Sometimes it didn't matter if you worked hard or not. They had their favorites, so I tried harder, but they let me go, so I had to find another job. I needed a place to stay. I went around and applied for jobs. Joe would watch Matthew while I went out to look for a job. One of the companies called the next day and interviewed me and gave me the job. I started working a few days after the company hired me. It was a housekeeping job at a hotel. My first day at work, one lady from Ghana was training me. We were cleaning the lobby restroom, and what I saw wasn't nice. It was disgusting. I couldn't even finish my day. I told them I was sick. I went home and never went back.

Kim was mad that I quit the job and told everyone not long before I got another job that the job I found was packing chickens. Some parts of the plant were cold, and some of it was hot. We packaged chicken, and they moved me around a lot. I hated the cold area, and the hot area made me sick because it was too hot, and I felt like passing out. I didn't have a choice, so I continued to work there while I looked for an apartment.

I found a place in Hamilton, Ohio, that had one bedroom and one bathroom. It was small, but we managed. It was only me and Matthew, so the rent wasn't expensive. Water and heat were not included. Evelyn sent me money to pay for the security deposit and the first month's rent. I told Kim I was moving out, and she said okay. The day came for me to move out. I was so excited, but scared at the same time. The unknown could have killed me, but I preferred to be on my own rather than stay another day with Kim. I had so many issues with the 1990 Nissan Sentra that Kim's husband sold me. The hardest part about the car was that when you stopped at a red light, the engine stopped, and you had to turn the engine off and turn it back on. It was so frustrating that I paid $1,500 for such a car.

My niece also loaned me money, but after I moved out, Kim said I stole the money. She was using my niece so much by requiring that she cleaned the house, cooked, did laundry, and cleaned the kids' room. Then she went to work and came back and still did cleaning. With Kim's husband, she did not get rest, and she still had to pay $400 rent. I called my other sister, Lisa, who is my niece's mom, and told her what was going on, thinking she could talk to them, but I was wrong. I told my sister Isla not to tell Kim I told her, but she did. Kim called me and said that as long as she existed, I was dead to her. She went on and said that I was evil, and I had an evil spirit in me. She said if someone doesn't want you as a sister, you don't want them as well, and I was dead to her and should never ever call her again. She hung up the phone; for some reason, I did not cry. I guess I was getting stronger.

Joe and some other friend helped me with some things for my apartment like pillows, comforters, dishes, and so forth. We didn't have a bed or couch, so at bedtime, I would use a lot of the comforters and lay them on the living room floor. I would make Matthew's side comfortable, and I would sleep by his side with nothing but the floor. I hated my job; if was not too cold, then it was too hot. I was always getting sick.

I made a new friend whose name was Jackson. He was very nice and said if I ever needed anything, I should let him know. However, when it comes to men and their help, I get worried because each time a guy went to help me, either he liked me or he would rape me. These things were in the back of my mind, and I knew America was not different from Ghana. We exchanged numbers, but I was not fond of the man. I kept telling myself I needed another job, so I went to the agency, and they gave me another temp job; this one was packing, but it was not hard. I started working, and the pay was $9 per hour. My babysitter and I became friends; she and her husband were very nice and were from Ghana.

When I wasn't working, I would go and hang out at their house. I told Kim's husband to give me back my money so I could get another car because the car broke down on me, and I wasn't able to drive. I made a few friends at my new job, so they would pick me up and drop Matthew off at the babysitter's house and take me to work. I was feeling that I was inconveniencing them. My friend Jackson had two cars, and he loaned me one car. I was able to use it to go back and forth to work.

My friend told me about this place called Rent to Own where you could get furniture and pay for it monthly, so I went and got a bedroom set, a couch, and a dinner table. I was paying $1500 a month because I didn't want my son to be sick from sleeping on the floor. I was so wrapped up with everything that was going on in my life that I forgot about James. He didn't call or send money. I wasn't sure about where our relationship status was, and I wasn't worried about it. I was worried about my son.

My babysitter sister was also from Ghana, and we became friends. She was working at a good company where they start the pay at $11.50 an hour for the third shift. I asked her to get me in, and she said okay. One Saturday, my friend Joe called and said he wanted to come visit. I said okay. Matthew was sleeping. Upon his arrival, he asked where Matthew was. I said sleeping. He then started touching himself. I ask him what he was doing. He said he wanted me. I asked him to leave my house. He asked why I thought he was helping me do so many things. He said he did it because he liked me and he wanted to date me. I told him I wasn't interested in him, and I have said thank you already for all the help you gave me and my son. If that wasn't enough, then I'm sorry, but you need to leave. He did. I was shaking and very scared. I thought he was going to rape me. It felt like history was going to repeat itself. I don't understand how any man who would try to help me would try to rape me at same time.

It was really hard for me to trust people. After Joe left my apartment, I never saw him or spoke to him again. My babysitter's sister got me a job at her company. It was also a warehouse job, but the pay was great. A few days later, I started my new job. I was still using my friend Jackson's car. My old apartment wasn't in a good neighborhood, so when I started making a little bit of money, we moved to a good neighborhood. I changed babysitters for Matthew, and one night on my way to pick him up, I had a car accident. My friend Jackson's car was totaled and I didn't have a driver's license, so I got a ticket. My friend said as long as you are okay, don't worry about paying for the car. Jackson went to court with me and paid my court fees and was such a wonderful person.

Jackson was very nice to me and Matthew, and my intentions were clear. I never thought he liked me, but I would find out soon. He would come over and play with Matthew, and if I needed anything fixed, he would fix it. He would invite me and Matthew over, and he would cook for us. He was really nice, and he was going above and beyond. Because I had been through so much, I wasn't thinking. Nobody had ever been nice to me without trying to take sex from me.

My guard had always been up, wondering why he was too nice. Could it be that he wanted something in return? In the back of my mind, I kept hoping I was wrong. My old babysitter's husband tried to sleep with me. He wanted to have a secret relationship with me, and I said no. They were friends with Kim and her husband.

I still didn't have a car, and I needed a co-signer for me to get a car, so I asked my babysitter. She said to ask her husband, so I did. He said he would if I slept with him. There was no way that I would do such a thing; I had been through enough with men. He went ahead and got the car. That was my second car, but this one was a new car. After he co-signed, I told him thank you. He was expecting more, but I told him I would not sleep with a married man, not in this lifetime. I told him I would never forgive myself if I ever tried that and that I'm not a girl who sleeps around with people's husbands. He was disappointed, but I didn't care. I got a new car; that was what mattered to me.

I was having immigration issues, so Jackson drove me and Matthew to Louisville, Kentucky. He was so kind and sweet to me and Matt. He never asked me to pay for the damage to his car, but I knew that the things he was doing for me were not free. I knew it was coming, but I wasn't sure how soon it would be. At the back of my mind, I thought nothing was free—not for me. I had to fight for my life and everything else. One morning, he came to my apartment and told me how he felt about me.

He said he was helping because I was a single mom, and he was also hoping that we could be together. I wasn't shocked or surprised. I already knew that was coming. My whole life had been like that. People who tried to help me or pretended to help me, either male or female, always wanted something from me in return.

It felt like a curse to me sometimes. I told him that I was sorry, and I didn't feel the same way about him.

My feelings for men were very small; sometimes I wondered why I'm not into men. Deep down in my heart, I knew why, but I still wondered. I was not into girls, either. It was like my feelings for men were dead. It was very challenging for me to tell him no. I think I hurt his feelings because he said he couldn't be my friend and that I should give him time. Meanwhile, though James and I didn't see eye to eye, he surprised us with a visit. When I saw him, I wasn't sure how I was feeling. At that point, my feelings for men were dead and buried. That evening, he wanted to have sex after not caring about Matthew and me, so I lied and told him I wasn't feeling well. He was understanding, but deep down in my heart, I didn't love him anymore. I kept telling myself that I could try. I felt bad, and I didn't want him to think that after he spent so much money by bringing me to the US. I left him, so I kept trying, but it was a hard thing to do. After James left, things were never the same again. I think he knew that my feelings for him had changed.

CHAPTER 11

UNBREAKABLE

Not long afterward, James traveled to Ghana to visit his family. When he got back, Kim's husband told me that we should try and make things work for the sake of the child we had, so I agreed to try. Kim's husband called James on the phone, and he spoke with him about us. James told Kim's husband he didn't want me anymore and that if he added a million dollars to me, he still didn't want me. I had a hard time with his rejection; I didn't take it too well. Even though I didn't love him anymore, I was still hurt by his words. I was hurt because of the words he used.

His words hurt me so much that it affected me emotionally and mentally, not because I was in love with him, but because I had considered trying. I was really hurt. I told Kim's husband to let it go and that I was okay. Kim and I were on speaking terms again. I wasn't sure if was sisterly love or if she just wanted to be in my business. I continued living my life. It was very hard for me. Jack and I hadn't spoken for a long time. With everything I was going through, I lost sight of him. I missed him, and I needed him in my darkest hours and time.

Matthew was only two years old, and he had been through so much with me. I didn't want this hard life for him. I didn't want him to experience what I had experienced in life. I wanted to give my son a better life than what I had when I was growing up. I was still working third shift, which was really hard. When I got off work, I would pick him up from the babysitter's house, give him a bath, feed him, and turn on the TV for him, and I would sleep next to where he was sitting. While I was asleep, he would get up and walk around the house. I knew that because things would be everywhere when I woke up. One day, I found him by the stove. He was holding a fry pan, trying to fry an egg. I guess I had being sleeping for a long time.

My baby was hungry, and he was trying to cook something for himself. I did realize that this had been hard on him, as well. I felt so bad and so sad; I felt like I had been a bad mom, but I was trying my best. This was not the kind of life I wanted to give him. How was I supposed to do this, being a mom? How could I become a good mom? All I could do was my best, because there's nothing like a good mom.

Only my best would be enough. I had learned that I could only try my best. I had made so many mistakes as a mom, and I learned from them as I went. Sometimes I made the same mistake over and over. I guess that was the only way I could learn. One evening, a friend and I were dropping Matthew off at the babysitter. We were running late for work, so I was speeding, which I didn't realize. All I could hear was the police siren behind us; we were stopped by the police. I stopped my car slowly, and I turned around. Matthew was in his car seat, but he didn't have his seatbelt on. I turned around to see the police officer who was walking toward my car and said, "Baby, please put your seatbelt on. Hurry up."

She was close; I slowly rolled down the window. The moment she got to the window, Matthew said, "Mommy, mommy, I did it! I put on my seatbelt." I almost peed on myself. I thought, *This is it; she would get me under child endangerment.* The police lady heard Matthew, and she laughed so hard. She looked at him and said, "Did you know that you were going 40 mph in a 25-mph zone?"

I said, "I'm sorry, officer. I did not realize it."

She kept smiling and said, "I will let you off with a warning today." I thanked the officer, and Matthew did, too. She smiled and said, "You're welcome."

James and I hadn't spoken in a while, and I was doing all I could to give my child the best life. I couldn't trust anyone; every man who came into my life to help me ended up wanting something that my heart, body, and mind didn't want to give. I had been so disappointed so many times by either my family members or people who I called friends. I was a good person, but people were not treating me that way. I learned the hard way that I could not always count on others to respect my feelings, even if I respected theirs, and that being a good person didn't guarantee that there would be good people in my life. I could only have control over myself and how I chose to be as a person. As for others, it is up to them to decide who they want to be as a person and how they want to live their lives.

I had a big heart; I sometimes fell in love hard. I missed people hard, I believed hard, I hoped hard, and I loved even harder. That gave everyone the biggest chance to take advantage of the fact that I let people in easily. I trusted too easily, and my doors were wide open. I thought highly of people, and I believed every word they said to me. I had the highest of expectations. Why? I am still trying to figure that out. I'm a mess, but I'm a beautiful mess. As I fought through this life, I was taking every punch, kick, claw, bite, and slap with a smirk, hoping one day I would find my happiness and my happy ending. God makes all things possible. I could do this. I'd come this far. I could handle the rest after having been orphaned, kicked out of the house in the rain, and raped by a family member, supposed friends, and strangers.

I have had nowhere to go or sleep at night, and I have been out there in the cold with no one to care for me. After all this, I can handle whatever life might throw at me. I kept telling myself that life is hard, but when Matt would sleep, I would watch him and cry. I told myself I had to be strong for him; he needed me, so I couldn't give up. I would keep fighting and working harder to give him a better life—the life I never had.

Meanwhile, James hadn't come to visit his son or called to check on him. I called James and asked him to pick his son up and spend time with him. He said he didn't have a babysitter. I told him he could find one like everybody else does. He said he would see what he could do. All I wanted was for him to be in his son's life, but that seemed too hard for him to do. He didn't provide food, clothes, insurance, or even money to help raise his son; none of that mattered to him.

While I was at work, I made a lot of friends, both male and female. I became friends with Lucas, my boss at work. Somehow, married men are attracted to me. I can't explain it. I don't understand it. I think they knew how vulnerable I was, so they were using my vulnerability. My boss and I become very close; he talked to me about his marriage. I have an effect on people, and they trust me and talk to me about their problems. People at work were talking.

Most were from Ghana. People from Ghana like to gossip and talk behind your back. My friend Sophia was my old babysitter's sister, and she helped me find the job. She was very upset that Lucas and I were close. She liked him, but I didn't know at that time.

My intentions were different. I saw Lucas as a friend. I wasn't sure how he saw me, but my co-workers were talking behind my back, including people I called my friends and trusted. Sophia and I got into a big fight. I had met a man a while back. He owned an African market, and he wanted me to work for him before I got the job at the warehouse. I was staying with Kim at that time, but Kim told me not to work there, and she went behind my back and asked the man to give the job to my niece. I was okay. I wasn't mad at all, but I kept forgetting that none of my sisters or brothers had my back or loved me the way I loved them. That was why I felt God was being so good when I got the job at the warehouse. It paid more than the man who owned the market was going to pay me.

Lucas and I continued to be friends. Sophia was my friend, so I told her everything. Lucas bought a washer and dryer for my apartment. He bought things for me and my son. At the back of my mind, I knew that all the nice things he was doing were not for free, and it was just a matter of time before he would try to have sex with me. Each time he called, wanting to come over, I pretended to be sick; that was the only way he wouldn't ask me for sex. He asked me why I was always sick. I told him I didn't know.

One evening, I was watching TV when he called and said that he wanted to sleep over at my apartment. I asked him about his wife, and he said she was traveling, and he didn't want to sleep alone. I said okay, but as soon as I hung up the phone, I turned off my phone and went to sleep. Forty-five minutes later, he came and knocked on my door, but I did not open it. I must have fallen asleep. After a while, when I woke up, it was past 2 a.m. I looked through my window, and he was still there, sitting in his car. I said to myself, "There is no way that I'm going to sleep with him." I went back to sleep, and the next time I opened my eyes, it was 7 in the morning.

The funny thing was that he never left. I turned my phone on and I saw eleven voicemails, so I called him because I felt bad. He said he had been knocking on my door. I told him I was sorry and that my medications must have made me fall asleep. He was so mad, and he said, "I know you don't like me the way like you, and I am done."

I asked him, "You are done because you wanted to sleep with me, and I don't want to, so we can't even stay friends?" He said no and left.

I gave him time because he was so upset; a few days later, I called him, and he answered. I asked him if he had calmed down. He said he meant it when he said that he was done. I said, "If it would make you feel better, go buy condoms and come over." I would drop Matthew off at the babysitter's. Deep down in my heart, I didn't mean it. I wasn't going to do that. He was upset about me saying that. I told him I thought that was what he wanted, so I would give it to him, but he said bye. I felt free for some reason. A few days later, his store number was calling, so I answered it. It wasn't him; it was his wife. I was surprised because she and I were not friends.

Why was she calling me? I asked her, and she said her husband said he loaned me $800, and she was calling to get that money back. I was so confused. I said to her, "With all respect, what money?" She said the money her husband had loaned me. I asked her whether she knew her husband liked me, and that was the reason he gave the money and all other things he did for me.

She said, "I don't care; I need that money back." I asked her if she knew her husband was at my house the other night. I told her that he only told her because I would not sleep with him, and that made him mad, so he told her.

I told her I'm not trying to be mean, but she should not call me again. I didn't owe him anything. I said to her, "Did you think that all the man did was take something from me? Did he call me back to give me back my innocence or back my life?" I felt strong for some reason. I told her, "You are married to the man, but you don't even know him. I'm young enough to be his daughter, yet he was trying to take advantage of me. That is what the man did. Please don't call me again. Talk to your husband. Goodbye." After about an hour, Kim was calling me. I answered, but I already knew why she called me. It was because she doesn't call me without a reason.

Kim said to go pay them their money. I said, "What money?"

She said, "They will take you to court if you don't pay them back."

I asked her, "Did you tell them to do that, or is that what she told you? You told them, didn't you? Also, they would have to prove the loan agreement to the court. When he gave me the money, he never said it was a loan. If he had had sex with me, do you think he would have told his wife, or you?" I was waiting. I told Kim to leave me alone. I was tired of people trying to help me so they could take something from me. Kim did not say anything else; she hung up. None of them has called me again.

When Sophia and I got into a fight because she wanted Jackson but he wasn't interested in her, she got mad. She thought it was because of me. I told her we were just friends and that I wasn't interested the way they all thought. She started calling me names, but I walked away. After work was over in the morning, I was walking with one of my friends to the parking lot. Third shift was over, and first shift was coming in. When I got to the parking lot, Sophia was standing there. I wasn't sure why. I thought the misunderstanding we had was over, but I was wrong. It was like I'd done something more than what I thought it was about. She called me every name, saying I had a kid with no husband and that no one wanted me. My friends didn't want me, and my baby's father didn't want me. She said I slept with men for money. She said I slept with Lucas for money. That was when I lost it. I told her to look at herself before coming for me, and that even if no one wanted me, God did want me, and that I have never slept with any man for money.

It was so bad that everyone was watching because I am a very quiet and shy person. I don't say much. It was as if she was ready to fight me. My friend told me to walk away, so I did. I went home. Sophia's sister used to babysit Matthew; not only that, but her husband was a co-signer of my car. They said I started the fight, and they wanted to take his name off the car. I told them I couldn't do that until the car was paid in full. They said what if they told the police the car had been stolen? I told them to go ahead and do that and that I'd tell the police they stole the car. Sophia and I didn't speak after that; at work, they separated us. She was working in a different department, and they had me stay in my department.

After a while, people were talking about how Jackson and I were close. It began to annoy me because they said I was sleeping with him, but the truth was that we were just friends. I told myself that I might as well do it, so they can have something to talk about, so Jackson and I began to have relations. We had lunch together, we hung out after work together, and now they had something to talk about. I didn't care anymore. I was having fun. Deep down in my heart, I knew what I was doing was wrong because he was a married man, but I couldn't stop. In time, I fell in love with him. I told myself it was bad, and I never brought him around my son.

That was because I wasn't sure how things would end. I knew it would end badly, and I still didn't care. As time went on, Jackson began to play games with me. He would talk with every girl at work to see if I would get mad at him, which I did. So, I began to play the same games with him. I would talk to every guy at work to make him mad, and he would get very upset at me. I didn't care. We had relations for about three hours. I worked there on and off, and one day he told me that he was not only cheating on his wife with me, but he was also cheating on me with another girl, and she was pregnant with his child. My heart broke, and I cried. I was hurt so badly. I couldn't believe it. I asked him why he did that, forgetting that he did the same with me to his wife.

Not long after he broke the news to me, I got fired. After that, I didn't hear from Jackson or see him anywhere. I filed for unemployment. I took a CNA class. It was really hard not having a job, and James wasn't supporting me in any way. My unemployment was denied. One of my friends was helping me with money and food, and I got a lawyer to appeal my case. I moved to another apartment because my neighbor was complaining about my son jumping, and I wanted to move. After I moved, I realized it was too expensive, so I asked the apartment office if we could move to a one-bedroom. They said no, so I broke my lease, and we moved to a two-bedroom apartment closer to my cousin. I thought I could afford it, but when the electric bill came, it was through the roof; the bill was $300. I could not take it anymore.

I rented my bedroom set and dinner table and flat-screen TV from Rent to Own, so when work got slow and I missed a few payments, I asked them to give me time. I was almost finished paying for it. One morning, they came and got everything. I had just made a payment of $200, but they didn't care. I was very upset. We ended up with nothing. I lost everything.

We had one of the old black-and-white TVs James had given me when we moved to Ohio. Sometimes you could only hear sound but no pictures, and we had to hit the side and the top for the pictures to come on.

I looked in the newspaper, and I found a duplex with two bedrooms and one bath and a yard. It was cheap, so we broke our lease and moved in. My new neighbors brought me candles to welcome me to the neighborhood. They were so nice and sweet. A few days after we moved in, I asked my new neighbor if she could babysit. Vicky started babysitting my son, and we became friends. She lived with her husband and grandson. After we had been living there for a while, she started calling me her daughter, and I called her mother. Her daughter started staying with her, and she and I became friends. After a while, I we started calling each other sissy. We became very close, like a family.

After I got done with my CNA class, I got a job as a home health aide. The first woman I worked for was highly functional. She called me the devil because I didn't want to go to church. I didn't want to go to church because she would not leave after church was over. She would cry and tell the pastor to pray for her, which is not a bad thing, but she became too much to bear. Her apartment was full of bedbugs. At first, I didn't know what they were. I only worked weekends, on Saturday and Sunday. When I got home, Vicky asked me what that bite was on my neck. I wasn't sure, so she checked and said it was a bedbug bite. I had so many bites on my neck, and it was becoming very itchy.

When I went back to work, I paid attention. This time in the night when there was no light, I saw them on everything in her apartment. My client's name was Lindy, and she was full of life and a drama queen as well. She was sixty-five years old and acted up when she wanted to have her way. When she couldn't, she would sleep on the floor and make a scene for everyone to see.

I told the office about the bedbugs, and they told me the other lady I worked with didn't complain, and I was the only one complaining. They said until the other lady complained, there was nothing they could do. It made me want to quit the job. One afternoon, my client asked me if we could go to my house and hang out, and I wanted to check on my baby. I missed him, so when we were going there, my client asked me to get her Wendy's. After buying the food, she attacked me because I got the wrong food, so I quit.

Life was not easy. Some days were better and some were not, but I still held on to hope and faith. If I didn't have anything, at least I could have hope. No one could take that away from me. What kept me going was the thought of my son and his unconditional love. No one else has ever given me anything like that.

After leaving my other job, I got a job like the first one, but it was a little better. The house was very dirty. Each day when I would go to work, they would leave dishes in the sink and clothes all over the floor, which was annoying, so I would clean and wash the dishes. Every day, the same thing would happen. I felt more like a maid than a nurse's aide. Cleaning the house was not part of my job, but I did it anyway. It became too much, so I decided not to clean for them anymore because they didn't keep it clean.

My job as a home health aide was mostly helping people. Some of them took advantage of me, but I loved what I did. With time, I began to find myself after Jackson broke my heart. I hadn't dated anyone in a long time. I was focusing on Matt and myself. I worked a lot of hours, so I was making a lot to cover my bills and food. I never asked James for money.

After a while, I applied for Medicaid and food stamps. We got approved. After a few months, James called and said he received a letter from the child support office and asked if I had filed for child support. I told him no, but the office did because we get food stamps and Medicaid. He said if I withdrew, he would give me money every two weeks.

I accepted it and called the child support office to cancel, but they said they would cancel the food stamps. I told them okay, and he started giving us $300 a month. He started picking Matt up, but each time he picked him up for three days, he would deduct money from the amount he gave us every month. When I ask him about it, he would say, "Because I kept him for a few days." I let it go.

I didn't want to take child support because I felt like I owed James because he brought me to his country, so I wasn't going to do that to him. As time went on, he continued to take amounts from the money he agreed to give every week; each time he picked Matthew up, he would deduct from the check he gave me. If he picked him for a week, he would give us a smaller amount. He would buy one pair of shoes, one pair of shorts, and four shirts for Matthew.

I tried not to complain because I could take care of my son. Even though things were hard for us, I kept my head high. I didn't make friends with girls; all my friends were guys. I kept my friendships with them professional. I didn't cross the line. I knew some of my friends would have liked to be more than that, but I wasn't interested. People thought of me as weird, but I didn't care what people thought.

Every year, I claimed Matt on my taxes, but this time, before I could file taxes and claim my son, James beat me to it. I was so upset. I said "I never asked you for child support, and now you want to use him on your taxes?" I went and filed for child support. This time, I would not withdraw it. When he found out what I had done, he was very upset. After court, he came to pick Matt up, and he was so upset.

He said I was very ungrateful and selfish after everything he had done for me. He said I was a liar and a gold digger. He called me a bitch and a witch. He asked who I thought I was and said that I slept with men for money. He said he would kill my mom and dad. That was when I got really upset and told him that both mom and dad had died when I was little. I said that God knew my heart. "You have hurt me more than you think, and I don't owe you anything. I gave you a son; that is enough for me. You can call me all the names in the book, and it would not change anything."

He said, "Do you think you are beautiful?"

I looked at him and smiled and said, "I am beautiful, and you can hurt me all you want."

My life had been complicated, and sometimes I wondered why. My sisters and I had a very weird relationship. I kept my distance because I felt like no one loved me or cared about me, and they always wanted to know what was going on in my life. Knowing that, I told them exactly what they wanted to hear.

My babysitter Vicky, her daughter, and I became friends; we called each other sisters. She signed me up for Tinder. That's when I met this handsome guy, Peter. I was very honest and open, but he started with a lie. I always give people benefit of the doubt. I have a good heart, and I love very quickly and hard.

I liked Peter so much that things heated up quickly. He didn't have money or his own place, but I looked beyond all that. I did everything I could to help him get on his feet. After a few months of dating, we moved in together. I wasn't thinking, and I ignored all the signs. When we started dating, my best friend Ama told him not to hurt me because I'm a good person with a good heart.

He sometimes ignored my phone calls. Sometimes I wouldn't hear from him for four days, and then I got a text saying, "Is this Stella, and is your boyfriend Peter?" I answered yes, and the person said, "This is his sister, and he is in jail." My friend and I searched every jail and couldn't find him anywhere, so I went to his grandma's house, and lucky for me, his sister was there. I told them I was his girlfriend, and I got a text from his sister saying he was in jail.

His sister said someone was lying to me, and she never sent this message to me. They looked at me weird. I should have known. I think I knew, but part of me didn't want to believe he wasn't right for me. His family called him on the phone, but he said he didn't know anything about a text. He came over and said he was sorry, and I forgave him.

He had a daughter, but I never met her. He would tell me that he was having issues with his baby's mom, and he couldn't bring her home. Each time he had her, he would take her to his grandparents' house or his friend's house. I wasn't complaining, but I knew something was not right. I fell in love with him, so I wasn't sure what I was feeling. With everything I had been through, I didn't even know if what I felt was love or hurt. He would stay home for three days and leave for the rest of the three days. I hadn't met any of his friends. He told me his friends were busy. When he used my car, I would find a woman's hairpiece in the car, and I would ask him about it. He would say it was his father's wife's stuff.

There came a time when he didn't have sex with me. I asked not because I really wanted it, but because I thought that was how things were supposed to be if two people lived together. He would tell me he was having problems getting his thing up. I didn't care about sex. I didn't even feel a need for sex. I did it because I wanted to make him happy, but if he didn't want it from me, then I wondered where he was getting it from.

He was on my telephone plan, so I checked the bills, and I couldn't believe my eyes. One night, he was sleeping, and I took his phone. He was talking to six other women, and one of them was his ex. I saw the things they were talking about. He said how much he loved her and he would marry her, and to the other woman, he said how he'd gotten his dick sucked, and he would be back the next day. I was speechless. Deep down, I knew, but I didn't know that it was that bad. I saw photos of him and his ex and his friends going out so many different times. All the time he was supposedly gone to be with his daughter, he was with other women, and he took food from my house to her house. That night, I was up all night reading the messages, and my stomach hurt. I immediately wanted to use the bathroom.

I was shaking and crying while going through his phone. After everything I had done for him, this was how he would repay me? I paid $1,500 for him to reinstate his driver's license. I went to Kentucky with him to pay all his fines and took him in when he had nothing. I woke him up. I wanted to hear what he had to say. He told me he was sorry about the other women, but he owed his ex's dad money from a drug he used to sell him long time ago, and he was trying to repay him. This was the way to do that—by pretending to be with her.

I was so stupid, so I believed the lies he told me. I tried to forget what I had seen on his phone, but it was hard to let go. With time, nothing had changed. He would still leave for three days. I asked myself why I was still with him, but I didn't have an answer. Maybe I knew the answer to my question, but I just didn't want to admit it.

He came home one day, and he finished paying what he owed and they were done, but he would come home right after work and still leave for the weekend. He kept saying it was to see his daughter, so I put GPS in his car. Throughout the weekend, he was at his ex's house. I would drive by and see them. I asked myself so many times why I was still with him—maybe it was love. I'm not sure what it was. One day I found him in a motel, and that was it. I told him I was done. He pleaded and said he wasn't going to do that again and that he loved me.

So, I gave him a choice—either her or me. When we were home, he would be texting and not paying attention to me. He got angry because I was asking him too many questions. He would break things in the house, such as my glass table and the glass in front of the stove, and he even pushed the long dresser to the floor and told me to clean it up. He said he got angry at me because he loved me too much and that he loved me until death. I got really scared. He never hurt me, but the way he looked at me when he began to break things around the house was frightening. My son was not home to see some of his behavior.

I wasn't sure why it took me too long to notice he never hung out with my son and called him boy. I needed a man who would love me and my child. If a man doesn't love your child, then you have to let him go. I asked him why he called my son boy when he has a name and why he didn't hang out with him and why he didn't do anything around the house. I would cook, clean, do his laundry, fold it, and put it away. I did everything a girlfriend is supposed to do, but I never got anything in return.

I kept telling myself that what we had was love. Matthew was a very shy kid; he didn't ask for much, and he didn't talk much. He didn't complain, either. I wasn't paying much attention to my son, and I didn't recognize it. I was too much into this man and his looks. He was six feet, three inches tall with light skin, and very handsome. The idea of me saying "my man" was the attraction. I don't think it was love that I was feeling; it must have been some-thing else. I asked myself why I was with him, and I didn't have an answer to that. Maybe I knew what the answer was, but I just didn't want to admit it.

I was in an unhealthy relationship, but I didn't care. He treated me very badly, and he acted mean toward me. He would go out and come home the next day and act as if everything was okay, and I continued to accept his behavior and still think he loved me. He didn't give me money for any bills, and on top of it all, he didn't have sex with me for months. I didn't care; I didn't have any feeling when it came to sex. I did it just to make my man happy, but he didn't even ask for it.

After being together for three years, I hadn't met his daughter. He continued to tell me how his baby mother didn't approve of his daughter spending the night at our house, and she didn't like me, either. I couldn't meet any of his friends, either, because they were busy with work. I was not sure what kind of relationship we were in. He always said how much he loved me, but it came to a point where I knew how he felt about me, and I was still trying to work it out. I would sometimes cry because I didn't feel happy, and I asked myself why. Each time, I ended up with the same answer.

After I put GPS in his car, I knew where he was at all times, and each time, he lied to me about where he was. One morning, he found the GPS in his car, and he was so mad. I told him I did that because he also lied to me. After that, he came home early sometimes, but some days, he came home when we were already in bed. When I refused to talk to him, he would act like a kid, breaking my things and following me around the house and calling me names at least ten times

On Christmas, he said he would try to make things right, so he asked me to come with him to his grandparents' house for Christmas dinner. When we got there, I felt a bit uncomfortable. One of his family members asked him where his girlfriend was, and he said, "That is her right there." She said no, that wasn't her, and they kept going back and forth. His cousin described the girl and how she looked. I felt stupid and sad. I immediately said to him that I wanted to leave and that I would come back for him when he was ready to come home. I left with tears in my eyes, and when I got home, I cried and cried. I now knew I wasn't the only woman he had been with and that everything was a lie.

After a while, my boyfriend called me to pick him and his brother up. With my kind heart, I went to pick him up, but on the way home, I was quiet. He was asking me what my problem was and why I looked so mad. He was pretending like nothing had happened earlier. On that day, I told myself I had to end this toxic relationship and I needed to be a good mother to my son and pay more attention to him.

I missed my best friend, Jack. I called him, and I told him what happened. He said, "You need to let him go." Jack told me that if a man loves you, he would do whatever it took to make you happy, and he would not make you cry. But if he is sleeping around and not giving you much of anything, then you need to let him go. I told him that I knew that, but it was hard because after being with a man for so long, even if he didn't love me, the feelings didn't stop. I didn't know what I felt for so long. My heart was heavy and sad, and everything had been taken away from me.

I didn't get the choice to grow like the rest of the kids out there. I was my own mother and father at the same time. I stopped worrying about this man; he never invited me to hang out with him and his friends, and he always made up things about why we couldn't hang with his friends, but I found pictures with him and his ex and his friends hanging out. If he was not home, he was with her. I got tired of it; I couldn't take it anymore.

I signed my son up for basketball and soccer. I was doing more for my son and me. I put him first, before anything else; that was how it was supposed to be. After a few days, he recognized that I had changed, so he began to come around. He would show up to my son's basketball game, and he would go church with us. He spent time with my son. Things had changed; it felt different. We started to get along, and we started talking about buying foreclosed houses and flipping them. However, I didn't trust him enough to put money into a business, and I was not sure where this is going.

Meanwhile, my relationship with Matthew's dad, James, was on the rocks. He was so disrespectful to me, but I never said anything bad to Matt about his father. I wanted his father to be in his life. I never wanted to be that person who kept him from his dad, and I didn't want him to grow up and blame me for anything. I wanted him to be the happy kid, but James kept putting things into my son's head every time he picked him up. He was trying to find out how my love life was going, and I never asked about him about his because I didn't care and it was not my business to know. However, James had to know about what was going in my life. James told my son how he brought me to America and I left him, but that was far from the truth.

I tried so hard to make James happy, but I think the case was that we didn't know each other enough and that we were two different people, or maybe I fell out of love with him before I came to America. I'm not sure what it was, but deep down in my heart, I wasn't planning to leave him. I was going to stay with him no matter what, but James changed. People change, but not always for the better. He was once a good man, and I think somewhere in there, he still is, but I don't see it.

The disrespect became too much. Each time I said something to him, he took it the wrong way. I think he was mad at me because he thought I never loved him. I think that I did love him, and I wanted to stay, but things had changed. I blamed him for my medical issues; he made me have an abortion in Ghana, and another after I had my son. I went through day-to-day pains, and I bled fifteen days in a month. I was in pain during sex, but the doctors couldn't find what was wrong with me. Each time I was in pain, I was mad at him. He took something from me that I could never get back. I tried to do the co-parenting thing with him, and I can give him much respect when it comes to our son.

When he picked Matthew up, I allowed him to come in the house. After leaving my apartment, he changed and got really upset. He thought I was using this money to buy things for my apartment, but it was my hard work. He didn't know how hard I had worked. I wanted to make sure my son didn't go through what I had been through. I wanted to give my son the best of the best. I wanted to be the best mother I could be, but sometimes I felt like I failed him. I tried to spend a lot of time with him. I tried my best not to fail him. I wanted to give my son the world. I had never learned how to ride a bicycle or play a video game, so I was trying to give my son everything I never had.

I had been spending too much time being a girlfriend and not enough being a mother, and I told myself I was doing my best. It wasn't good enough; I should have tried harder and put my son first. As time passed, my relationship with Peter became better, so I thought we would travel to Chicago and stay in a hotel. We had so much fun, but once we got back home, everything was different. He spent more time with his dad than with my son, and when he was home, he was either on his phone, or he would fall asleep watching TV.

He told me that he hated to go to the movie theater, and he hated to watch long movies. I didn't understand why. I would ask him why, and he would try to explain it or get mad. He said he was trying his best to work on his relationship with me. However, each time we talked, I began to realize that he was a broken person before he met me, and I was trying to fix him and change him. I began to understand why he cheated, which didn't make it okay, but I tried to understand him.

I told him that we needed a break from each other and that he needed to find himself and figure out what he wanted out of life. I told him that he needed to love himself first before he could love someone else. I told him I had been nothing but a good woman to him, and I need to be treated right, with respect and love. I packed him a few clothes, and he left after a few days. I spent time with my son. He was happy to be just the two of us, but I was missing Peter so much that after a week, I asked him to come back home and told him that I missed him. He wasn't ready to come back.

It looked like he liked being single. I insisted that he must come back. He was so mad at me, but he did. I told him he needed to pay some part of the bills at the house, so each time he got paid, I collected some part of the phone bill and money for groceries. It made me feel better; I wasn't feeling used or taken advantage of. He was still not having sex with me, which made me feel like he was still cheating on me, even though I didn't care about the sex. I put a recording device in his car. I know how this may sound like I was crazy, which I'm sure I was, but I didn't care. I needed to find out. I needed to know. Each time he left the house and came back, I would find a hairpiece in my car or something that didn't belong to me. He would tell me it was for his dad's wife.

I didn't get it, but he would get upset and break things in the house. He never tried to hurt me or my child, but I didn't want my son to live in that kind of environment. In time, things became different and weird. I started working two jobs: first I would be in the factory from 11 p.m. to 7 a.m., and I would come home, get my son ready for school, and sleep for a few hours. Then I would go to my second job as a home health aide from 2 p.m. to 9 p.m. It was really hard on Matt. I felt like I was a bad mom. I would sleep a lot because I was always tired.

Meanwhile, I had been experiencing some health issues. I felt like I was being punished for something I did. Day in and day out, I was having all kinds of health problems. I got more worried; I didn't want anything to happen to me. I wanted to grow old and watch my son finish college and see my grandkids. The doctors couldn't find anything wrong with me, but deep down, I knew something was wrong. I continued to take things one day at a time, knowing that with God, all things are possible.

People didn't understand why I was always sick. I didn't understand it, either, but it was not for them to understand or make sense out of it. I had very bad headaches, and I bled for fifteen days twice a month. I was so worried about my health that I couldn't eat sometimes. I couldn't sleep, and I was losing weight because I could not keep anything down. I still went to work, whether I was sick or not. I had to go. That was the only way I could pay my bills and feed my son. I sometimes took my son to work. My client's mom was so nice. They said I could bring him, which made things a lot easier for me.

Sometimes I left my son with Peter and some days I took him with me. However, in time, the relationship with Peter changed. We didn't see eye-to-eye, and I wondered what I was still doing with him. My neighbor, who I called Mom, loved me and my son like I was her own daughter. We lived close to each other, but after they moved, things became different. Matthew and I were doing okay.

After being with Peter for three years, I decided that it was time I let him go. I was not only hurting myself, but also my son, who is an amazing kid. He didn't complain about anything and was always smiling, no matter what.

Meanwhile, I decided to get baptized and start my life over by giving myself to God. It was an amazing experience. I would not change anything about that day. I felt new and clean. Giving my life to God was the best thing that could ever have happened to me. My friends and family were there, and it felt great. A few months later, I had Matthew baptized, too. He looked so happy, and our lives had changed for the better.

After a few months, Peter and I talked. I told him to move out, which was the hardest decision I had ever made in my life. I packed all his belongings and told him I was going out of town, and he needed to leave by the time I got back. A few days later, when I came home, he was gone. I cried myself to sleep because I missed him; it wasn't the same, even though he had been cheating on me. I said to myself that I loved him and questioned why he couldn't love me back. After being with someone for four years, you can't not love them. I loved him.

We decided to stay friends. It was hard at first. Matthew was with his dad, and when he came home, I asked him if he was okay with Peter being gone. Matthew and I started to develop a good relationship, and after some time, we worked out together, which was very nice. We talked every other day. I was working two jobs: my health aide job and a warehouse job. I wanted to give Matthew the best life I could possibly give him.

I decided that we should move. My landlord had a lot of houses, so I rented a three-bedroom house, and we moved. Matthew had to change schools; he hated his new school. He came home crying every day, which broke my heart. He said the bus driver has being mean to him. I called the school and told them to speak with the driver. I checked in now and then to make sure he was doing okay. I hated the night shift job.

After Peter and I broke up, I didn't wait to exhale; I jumped right into another relationship. I needed someone to help me heal from the pain Peter had caused me. It hadn't been a month, and I was seeing a new man. That was not like me, but there I was with Jose. He was nothing like Peter. He was not cute. He didn't have the looks Peter had, but he was caring and charming and giving. I never had to use my money to pay when we went out, and he bought me nice things. He gave me gifts, and he made sure I was okay. I felt special. Nobody had ever done that for me before, but I was about to discover the other side of Jose.

One day, he asked me if I could add him to my phone plan. I didn't want to, but he said he would pay my bill—he promised. I said okay, so I added him. Soon afterward, he borrowed my son's Xbox controller. One month passed and then two months. The phone bill was due, and he had still not returned my son's controller. I said to him that the phone bill was five days past due, and I asked him when he was going to pay that. He would not text me back or return my calls. Fifteen days passed, and still I hadn't heard from Jose. I sent him a long text, asking him to return my son's stuff, and the next day, he dropped it off in the mailbox while we were sleeping. My son never met him; I didn't like the idea of a man meeting my son until I was sure a relationship was going somewhere.

After he dropped off my son's controller in the mailbox, I asked him when he was going to pay the phone bill. He didn't respond, so I called the phone company and had him blocked, so he couldn't make or receive calls. The phone company said to cancel the contract, but doing that would cost me $400, so I took him to a small claims court. They sent him the papers at his home. That's when I knew who he really was. He texted me and called me all kind of names, and he said, "I know where you are living; I will find you."

I was scared for my life and had security cameras installed all around the house. If anybody rang my doorbell, I had to check the cameras before opening the door. I felt like a fool. I hadn't fully healed from Peter, and I jumped right into another relationship, thinking it would help me get over Peter. It was nothing like that. I was hurt twice. Jose paid off the phone, and I had to transfer his phone into his name after he said he would post all the naked pictures I sent him to the internet and show everybody. I said for him to go ahead and thank you for all the insults. May God bless you more and more. His text messages kept coming every day. I called the phone company and had him blocked, so he couldn't text me anymore.

I was terrified of Jose. I said to myself, "What I did I get myself into? I haven't healed." I was still hurt; now I was hurt even more, and it was worse than the first time. I was still missing Peter, but I was trying to get over him. I worked more, and I started to do more with my son to take my mind off things, which was hard to do, but I had to try.

I spoke with my cousin, and she had a friend who worked in the hotel to help me get a job there. I went down and applied for the job. I worked two weekends and three days on second shift. I loved my new job and made new friends. I worked three days at my home health job and four days at the hotel.

My cousin said we should go to Atlanta, but I wasn't sure if that was what I wanted to do. I agreed that we should go and see it, and then I could decide if I wanted to move or not. We set a date to go to Atlanta.

I got to Atlanta first. After I took shelter at the hotel, I met my new friend. She asked me which hotel I was going to. I told her, and it happened that we were both going to the same hotel. She was very nice. We exchanged numbers that evening, and we went out. She took me to the strip club; that was my first time being somewhere like that. It was loud, and I really didn't care for things like that. We had so much fun, and she didn't let me pay for anything. After being in town for a few days, I left to go back to Ohio. I was very upset that my cousin wasn't able to come, but I made a friend. Things happen for a reason.

Back home, Peter and I stayed friends. We talked every day. I thought that talking to him would help me get over him. I felt like I made a mistake by breaking up with him. I loved my new job, and my old job became too mentally draining for me. Too much was going on after my client lost her mom. She also lost her grandpa and grandma and had no one. I had worked with her for eight years, but I was getting tired of the job. I didn't want to give up on her because she was legally blind and had a brain of a two-year-old, although she was twenty years old. I loved her; she was a sweet and funny girl. I called her Sissy.

I was picking up the pieces of my life. I hadn't spoken to Kim for a while. She only called me when she needed me to go relax her kids' hair. She didn't call if she didn't need anything. As for Amelia, we talked every day. I felt she called to get information from me and take it to Kim. I told them exactly what they wanted to hear. I had a great relationship with Amelia's kids. They loved me and respected me.

A few years back, I visited Ghana. I hadn't been there for years. Matthew was five years old. It looked different, and everyone I knew looked different. I didn't have many friends there. Matthew didn't like it. He said it was too hot, which it was. I stayed with my other best friend, Bailey, but things didn't go well. We started fighting for no reason. Her mother was staying with her, and it made things a bit hard between my friend and me. It was very hot at night, and the room didn't have air conditioning, just a fan, and it didn't work well. Matthew had heat rashes all over his body. My best friend's mother was trying to cause a misunderstanding between us.

A few days later, I left to visit my other friend, with whom I stayed with in New York when I was pregnant with Matthew. We have been friends ever since. She welcomed me and Matthew with open arms, so we decided to stay with her in the hope that I could save my friendship with Bailey. When I told her we were going to stay with someone else, she was very upset, but I was doing the right thing. After moving there, she made me and Matthew feel comfortable, and we began to enjoy Ghana a little bit more. I called my other cousin from my dad's side. After all these years, I hadn't spoken with them. I forgave them for abandoning me. My friend and I went to visit, and they cooked for us. I didn't eat the food because I was afraid they would poison the food. I told them my stomach hurt, so I couldn't eat. They packed up the food for me to take.

They had not done anything nice for me, so why now? On our way home, I threw the food in the trash. I knew it was wrong, but I did it anyway. I told my friend I was not ready to die and leave my son. Back in the days when families arranged marriages, Dad arranged marriage for me and my uncle's son. I was young, and I didn't understand it. Dad always said he was my husband, but I didn't care about it. After Dad passed away, he was one of the people who raped me for the second time. He said, "You are my wife." I was shy and could hardy speak for myself. He took advantage of me, and after that, each time he came to town, he pretended as if he didn't know me. It hurt, and I felt sad without understanding why.

One day, he came to town and said, "This is my wife." He came with a woman. I said okay with a sad-looking face. They all treated me badly, so when I came back to visit in Ghana, he called and said, "This is your husband."

I said, "Who? I'm not married."

He said, "Don't be like that." He then asked me to come see him. I told him I couldn't, but if he wanted to see me, he was more than welcome to come to where I was. After I gave him the address, he never came.

Kim was in Ghana at that time. She had my nephew pick me and Matthew up, and we spent time together. We even slept in the same room and the same bed. We cooked and just talked. I said to myself that this was new. Kim had been really nice to me. I thought this was a start for us to start a relationship. I wasn't expecting anything from her, but I was hoping she would say she was sorry for all the pain I had been through. I was hoping that we could talk about the past, but it didn't happen.

My relationship with Kim during my stay in Ghana was very surprising, but at the time, I had my guard up because I wasn't sure what tomorrow would look like. We visited James' mom's house. She was really nice, too, and has been welcoming all the years that I have known her. James' whole family came. James' sister, who was my school mom back in the day, stopped talking to me when her brother and I ended our relationship. Everyone else was excited, but things were weird between me and her; we hardly said two words to each other.

I heard James got married after we broke up, but I wasn't sure if it was true or not. I didn't even care. I wasn't ready to get married because I had a hard time trusting people, and I'm not fond of men. My heart was heavy with so much pain, but I was learning to let things go. I was taking things one day at a time. After being in Ghana for six weeks, we came back to the United States. I continued to work as a home health aide and took care of my son.

Life was a little bit harder. One day, I fell asleep, and Matthew missed the school bus. I continued to do my best as a mother. Vicky and her family were very lovely. In the summer, I would grow a garden full of tomatoes, watermelon, okra, and peppers. I loved doing my gardening; it gave me something to do. Matthew and I went to church every Sunday.

I learned that life is how you define it. I prayed to God every day for giving us our daily bread. Hope and faith were what kept me going, and the thought of my son gave me strength to keep moving every day. I learned that it is not because things are difficult that we do not dare; it is because we do not dare that they are difficult. My understanding of life was different now. When I was fifteen years old, I had a favorite t-shirt that I wore every day. What made the t-shirt interesting was that it had "Life is a journey, not a destination" written on the front.

I continued to be a mom, and my relationships with my sisters were still the same; nothing had changed. Of the two of my sisters here, I only talked to one, and not at all with the rest in Ghana. I haven't spoken to any of my brothers in years. I don't even know what they look like. My sister Amelia always says to call the rest of my family, but I asked her, "Why should I be worried about them when none of them were worried about me?" I told her I'm happy keeping my relationship with fear away from them.

Kim called one morning, which surprised me because she never called me. She said, "I just got back from Ghana, and I was checking on you and Matthew." I said okay. I thought she was only calling to get information about what was going on in my life. She never cared before, so why now? I didn't believe her.

After my relationship with Peter was over, I moved away from the apartment we'd lived in. We moved to a big place. I didn't want to keep holding on to someone who didn't love me. I gave up, but deep down, I still loved him. He would call me sometimes, and sometimes he would text to say he was checking on me. I wanted closure, so I invited him over and asked him if he had ever loved me at all, because I gave him everything. I gave him my heart, my love, and my trust. He said, "I loved you, and I still do."

I said to him, "I don't believe you, because when you love someone, you fight for them. You don't let them go."

He looked at me and said, "I don't know how to fight for anything." Then he asked if we could still be friends, and I said yes.

We became friends, but I don't know why. I said yes to him, and he knew my weaknesses, and he knew I could never say no to him. I had a small car, so I sold it to him for $500. He was paying $100 a month, and I agreed to keep the car in my name, and the insurance, as well. After he was done with the payments, I told him to put the car and the insurance in his name. He agreed after I transferred the title to his name. I called the insurance to put the car in his name after I got another payment bill. He was supposed to call and make a payment, but he lied to me that he had called and made the necessary change. When I called him and asked why he lied to me, he got very defensive and began to be disrespectful to me by calling me a bitch and other names. I said to him, "Thank you, and may God bless you."

We never spoke again after I learned that if you lost it, it is because you were meant to find something better. Trust and let it go and make room for what is coming. I didn't really care about the relationship; it was just of having the idea of having someone in my life. In a few weeks, I felt free and happy. I wasn't holding back anymore. It was just me and my son and my job. I was working at the hotel and working as a nurse's aide. My son and my job were all I cared about. I didn't have time for a relationship, because I went from work to home and from home to work and Sunday church and my son's basketball games. I was trying to find myself—to find who I was, who I am, and what I was becoming.

My cousin said we should move to Atlanta. I didn't want to. Just the thought of starting over somewhere was difficult. I spoke with my son, and I asked him what he thought about us moving.

He said he was okay with it, so we went to Atlanta to look for an apartment and a school for him.

I didn't want his grades to go down. My son was an A student and was an awesome child. I couldn't ask for anything more. After we left Atlanta, I wasn't sure if I wanted to move from Ohio. I was scared of the unknown. When we got back, I continued my routine and being a mom. I wasn't sure if I wanted to move, but with time, my cousin convinced me that it would be good for me. I was worried about my son. He was the most important thing in my life, and his happiness mattered to me the most.

I told my friends and niece that I would be moving. I know she was not happy, but she expected it and said, "Whatever makes you happy. I will support you." I told one of our closer friends, and she was happy, but she said Atlanta was very expensive and that I shouldn't go, and that we are all happy here. She wondered why I had to go, but I had made up my mind to go, even though I was scared. I knew God was in control. Making a big life change is pretty scary, but regret is even scarier.

I decided to tell James. He came to pick up our son, and when they returned, I told him that I got a job opportunity, and we were moving to Atlanta. He was not happy and said he wanted Matthew to come live with him. I told him that would never happen and that he should give me a reason why he wanted him to come and stay with him. I asked him, "Why now, after all these years, after I have raised him, and he is all grown up and can do things for himself? Why would you want him now?" He said he would let the judge decide.

I told him if that was what he wanted to do, then I would be waiting on the court order. I told him I'm a great mom, and my son is on the honor roll, an A student. He is happy, and for James to get him, he had to prove me unfit. That was only way the judge would give him to him. He was very upset and said, "Do you think you are the only parent for him?"

I said, "Yes; for the past twelve years, I haven't seen you doing the father duty, and after all my hard work, now you want take over. That will never happen." He left after he called me a bitch.

I told my son how sorry I was. I wanted him to be happy, and if he wanted to stay with his dad, he could. He said, "No, Mom, I want to go with you, and not my dad."

We began to sell some of my stuff because we lived in a three-bedroom house. My friend Josh told me to start packing and not to wait until last minute. We packed all we could. I wanted to wait until my son was out of school. I felt bad because he was leaving all his friends behind. Even though he said he was okay, I still felt bad that my son was leaving his friends. He was willing to go with the flow and didn't complain much about anything. I had everything planned for the move, but hiring movers wasn't an option for me. They were too expensive. Betty said she and her husband would come from Tennessee and drive the U-Haul for us about a week before the moving date. I called Betty to confirm if they were still coming, but unfortunately, Betty said her husband had some tooth pain, so they couldn't come. I was a bit disappointed. I didn't have any other options, and I felt like it was a sign telling me not to move.

I began to ask around to see if I could find someone to help drive the U-Haul we rented. The twenty-six-foot truck was too big for me to drive. I asked Tom at work. I told him I would pay him $300, and he said yes. I was able to breathe and not worry anymore.

I was almost done packing when my landlord came and inspected the house, and she gave me a card that had a $10 gift card inside. I said to myself that was nice of her to do that, and she doesn't have to do that. She wished me well and said goodbye.

At the end of the day, all my friends came and surprised me. They helped me load the U-Haul, and it was very emotional for me. I couldn't have been more grateful for all the love they had shown me from the time we worked together. Then my friend from the hotel drove us to Atlanta. It was a challenge on the road; the U-Haul was driving very badly, and we spent more money on gas. It felt like we had been driving forever, and things didn't end there. We arrived on June 27, and the lease was not until July 1. I thought it would be ready when we got there, and we could move in instead of staying in a hotel. I had job interviews on Monday, and we arrived on Wednesday the week before.

When we got there, the apartment wasn't ready, so we stayed in a hotel for three days. When we finally got the key to the apartment, it was still not ready. They were now painting the apartment. After they left, the movers came and helped unload the stuff, and we put the rest in storage. We started unpacking, and we saw there were roaches in the apartment. We freaked out and went back to stay in a hotel for another day. I felt like it was a mistake moving there. I always to listened to my friends, but in this case, I shouldn't have listened to my cousin. It is not a bad thing to listen to family and friends, but sometimes you have to listen to your inner self.

The apartment manager and all the staff were very nice, and I was willing to work with them to resolve the issue, but it was really hard being at a place where you don't have any friends or family around. I began to hang out at the leasing office, and I made a friend there. She was really nice and sweet. I started to ask her how to find things around there. She then took us to her church; they were nice. I liked the church and felt comfortable there.

My boss from my hotel in Ohio called the hotel in Atlanta and got me a job. It was very nice of him to do that. I had an interview after we arrived in Atlanta. A few days later, my new boss told me I could start after a week. It was a relief that I got a job, but the pay wasn't what I was expecting. I thought it be would more, but the most important thing was to have a job.

We started unpacking our things, and I had to find a school for Matt. Matt and I planned to see the Coca Cola factory, the aquarium, museums, and Stone Mountain. We saw all these places in the week before I started working. It was beautiful, and my son was happy.

I had saved money, so I was able to pay my rent for three months, but my savings weren't enough to pay my other bills. I began to get worried. I applied for twenty jobs a day but got nothing. Some of the jobs called me for interviews, but they didn't pay much. I wanted higher pay, but they were lower, and I couldn't accept them. We didn't know anybody there. Atlanta was different from Ohio. Everything was expensive—maybe because I didn't have the money.

After a while, I got sick with a cold, and it became worse so that I wasn't able to go to work. My son was very worried about me, and he would come to my room and sit with me. He would sleep beside me and touch my head. He would bring me water and ask me if I needed anything to eat. He would ask me ten times if I was okay and check on me every five minutes. I have an amazing son; I couldn't ask for anything more. I still went to work while being sick; it wasn't easy. Things were harder in Atlanta than in Ohio. The rent was too much, and I had things in storage at the same time. I applied for any job I could think of, but all the job offers were for less pay than I was making.

My friends were telling me it had been a while since I went on a date, so they kept insisting I go on a date, even if it was a one-night stand. I kept telling them I didn't know how to do that; I wasn't the type of a girl who slept around with everyone. I was a very weird person. My yes's mean yes, and my no's mean no. I didn't sleep around, but they didn't get it. They didn't understand me. After everything I had been through, I had grown as a person, and I had learned so much from life. They didn't know me well and kept pushing, so I signed up on a dating site and started talking to other people. My first date was this guy who was six feet, three inches tall. I sat in my car thinking that if I didn't like him when he came out, I would drive off. Unfortunately, before I could drive off, my car stopped running and wouldn't start.

I went inside the bar, and we had a very nice conversation. I told him that my car had stopped. He helped me, and after jump-starting the car, he followed me to Auto Zone and made sure my car was running right. Before he left, he wanted to come to my house and watch a movie with me, but I told him no. I told him, "I don't just invite people I just met to my house." When it came to my son, I didn't do that. I told him we could go out, but I couldn't invite him to my house, and I had to be sure this was going somewhere before having him over. I told him it would take months. He said okay, but I never heard back from him again.

A few weeks later, another of the guys reached out on the same site. We first started texting and set up a time to meet. That morning,

I didn't want to go, but at the same time, I didn't want to hear my friends nagging me, so I went on the date. I introduced myself, and he introduced himself as well. I told him I couldn't eat early in the morning, so I had a hot chocolate, and we talked and talked. I always prayed to God to send me a wonderful man who would love me only and only have eyes for me.

Later that day, he texted me and asked if I wanted to come over. I wasn't sure why he invited me to his house, but I wasn't scared to go over to his house anymore. We watched movies and talked. He told me why he was single, and I told him about my old relationship. I was honest for the first time in a long time. I was truthful and honest, and I was very open about my past relationships. We both felt the connection that we had. I told him I wanted to take things very slowly, and he said he wasn't going anywhere and would be here as long as it takes. It was getting late, so I went home. We talked for the next few days. He asked me to come over again. I told him okay, but in the back of my mind, I knew I wasn't going to sleep with him anytime soon.

He texted me and asked me if I wanted anything to eat. I told him I was okay, but he insisted, so I said okay. When I got to his house, he had just gotten out of the shower. He hugged me, and he smelled so good. He poured me a class of wine. I don't drink, but I told him I could drink a little bit of sweet wine. I only drank a little, and we watched a movie. He couldn't stop looking at me. At the end of the movie, I left. Nothing happened because I wasn't ready for anything. He told me that he really liked me. He had three kids, both in college, and I told him I had one kid in middle school. He said he hoped I liked him back.

I told him how we had just moved there about two months before, and I didn't have any friends in Atlanta yet. He told me how he had moved there four years ago. I told him my job wasn't paying me well, and my rent was very expensive, and I was looking for a second job. He told me not to and that he got me. I told him that I wasn't used to a man taking care of me, and I had been independent all my life. He said, "This can be a start. I got you." I smiled at him. I wouldn't believe it until it happened. I didn't know how to ask a man for money. If I really liked you, I could never ask you for money, but if we started as friends, I would ask for it.

Meanwhile, I enrolled Matthew at school. It took a lot of paperwork to start at a new school. I was worried about him making new friends because he is a very quiet and very shy kid. We went to the open house, and he meet a lot of people. He looked happy, and everything went great.

My date, Mark, texted me and asked me if I wanted to go with him to his friend's girlfriend's birthday dinner. I said yes. I was happy to go out for the first time in a long time. He gave me the time: 7 p.m. I drove to his house, but when I got there, he wasn't there. I called him, and he said to go inside the house, and his son was there. I had met his son previously, and he introduced me to him, but I decided to stay in the car outside Mark's house because I was talking on the phone with my friends. Mark arrived shortly and came to my car. He said, "Why are you not in the house?"

I said, "Because I was on the phone."

He shook his head, and with a smile on his face, he said, "You are not normal."

I said, "Yes I am," with a smile.

He would not stop looking at me the whole way there. When we got to the party, he got out and opened the car door for me. No one had ever done that for me before. It felt great. He held my hand, and it felt good. I hadn't felt like that in a while. He held my hand while we walked into the restaurant. At the restaurant, he ordered my food and drink for me. I met his friend and his friend's girlfriend and other people. People were complimenting my dress and my hair. It felt great. The whole time we were there, he couldn't take his eyes off me.

There were a lot of beautiful women there, but he was looking only at me, and it felt amazing. Mark couldn't keep his hands and his eyes off me. I was a little tired because I had worked the night before. He saw how tired I was when we were talking. All the guys' eyes were on me. Mark than held my hands so tight. He walked to the car and opened the car door for me again. When we got to his house, we said goodbye. He opened my car door for me, and before I knew it, he kissed me. It felt good; we kissed for five minutes, and he left.

We texted back and forth a few times. All of a sudden, he stopped texting me. I would text him: no response. I would call him: nothing. I was very confused. I didn't understand why, or maybe I said something. I was hoping that as a forty-two-year-old man, he would at least text me back and say something like, "I don't think I can see you again." I really liked him. When I love, I love hard, and I was having hard time letting it go. I felt used and very disappointed. One of my friends at work was friends with Mark, so I asked her. I told her we went out few times, but he would wouldn't text me or call me back, and I was confused.

On Saturday, she called me and asked if I had time to talk. I said yes. She then said that she called him; he didn't answer, and she texted him. He called her back the next day, and she told him, "I met your girl." He said, "Which girl? She wasn't my girl; we only went out one time."

I said, "Wow, that's sad." He told her that me and him would never work out. I asked her why didn't he tell me this himself? Maybe he wasn't a man enough to speak up. I told her that was okay and that I believe things happen for a reason. God bless him, and I wish him nothing but the best.

Deep down, I was hurt, because that was the first time in three years I had opened up to someone, and I felt like a fool and felt so stupid and was really hurt and sad, but life must go on. After that things, weren't great. It was hard. I applied for jobs every day. I would apply for twenty jobs a day. A few called, but the pay rate was very bad. I was looking for jobs in downtown Atlanta, and the pay rate was very poor. Moving to Atlanta was one of the hardest decisions I have ever made. After we settled into our apartment, we continued to find roaches in the apartment. I tried to stay positive. I worked at night, and Matthew would be asleep before I left home. I had security cameras in the house so I could see what was going at home while I was at work. It was hard for me to leave him, but as a mother, I can only try my best.

I was so busy trying to figure out how to make this place work. Going back to Ohio wasn't an option. I was determined to make it work; life is not supposed to be easy. I had to make it work. Kim called me almost every month. I wasn't sure why she was calling. Most of the time, when she called, she asked how I was doing and how Matthew was. I would also ask her how her kids were doing.

The conversations were very weird. She said, "So when are you getting married, and when are you having another baby?" I said Matthew and I were doing okay, and I was okay with what I had. I wondered how this was any of her business. Why was me getting married and having a baby any of her concern? She only called me to find out what was going on in my life. I had never pick up the phone to call her for anything.

One morning, Kim called, and I didn't answer the phone. She left me a voicemail and said to call her. A few minutes later, I called her back. She said, "I went you to come work with me. Just get a contract for home health aide job. I want the money to stay in the family, so come work with me." I asked myself why she now wanted me around. What was she thinking? She thought I would pack all my belongings and my kid and move 485 miles just because she needed someone she could control. I told her I couldn't. I said if I was still living in Ohio, then maybe I would, but I would not move back. She said okay, and that she understood.

She said I would be paid $3,000 a month. I said it was never about the money. Even if my life depended on it, it would never happen; I would never work for her. Kim asked me how I was doing. She said I wish you were here so you can work with me and make that money. I said yeah, sure, but it was too late. I said I didn't want to work that kind of job again. It is very emotionally and mentally draining, and even if I was in Ohio, I didn't think I would have done it. I was expecting her to ask me to move, but that conversation never came up.

I guess this is what they do: my sisters are always about them— especially Kim. She wants people to be below her. She thought she would be the only sister who is making all the money. I didn't hurt her. I forgive them all, but I would not forget, and I told them what they wanted to hear so they would do their happy dance. Do I trust them? No, I would never trust them. Dad used to say that trust is like an egg you must hold onto; once it is broken, you can't pick it back up. None of them have ever apologized for not believing me or sorry for leaving me out there alone.

When I went to Ghana, I saw my other brother. He looked different; he was married with six kids. I wondered why, but everybody is different. I gave him some clothes and money. I didn't see him again before I left Ghana. He started to call me a few years later. First, when the call came, I wasn't sure who it was. He said his car had broken down, and also he wasn't feeling well. He was wondering if I could send him money. I told him I didn't have any money right now and that I would let him know if I could help. Then he would call me every week as if I owed him money. I was annoyed about number of phone calls I received from him in a week.

I decided to send him $50. I didn't have to, but I have a big heart, so I did. After I sent him the money, he never even called to say thank you. He didn't even ask me how my son was doing. All he cared about was the money. I felt angry. He never looked for me after Kim and her husband kicked me out. He never tried to make sure if I was okay or not, and now he was asking me for money. I have not seen my other brother since Mom died and I moved away with Dad. Even when I stayed with Kim, I never saw him again. We never spoke. I heard he was married and had a lot babies. That was all I knew about him.

My family only cared about themselves. I continued to speak with Amelia. I know each time I had a conversation with her, she called Kim and told her, but I continued to give her the benefit of the doubt, and she continued to share my conversations with Kim. I have never stood up for myself with my sister back in Ghana. We called anyone who was older than us sister or brother. You couldn't talk while a grown person is talking. You stood there and listened without a word. It was always like that. We were taught to respect our elders. Even when we were all grown up, it stayed the same.

My life in Atlanta wasn't easy. I guess life wasn't meant to be easy. You have to go through something bad to get something great. I finally got a second job. My schedule was very difficult. After my night shift, I went to my second job and worked another eight hours. I was hardly ever home, and each day I felt bad, but I wanted to give my son a better life—the life I never had.

It felt like I had been gone twenty-four hours, and when I get home, I only spent one hour with him, and then I went to sleep. I have the most amazing son. He never complains, and he is not demanding. I feel so blessed to have such a wonderful son. I couldn't ask for anything more. By the time I got home, he had finished his homework, and he'd eaten dinner. The first thing he asked me when I got home was, "Mom, are you hungry?" That made me feel happy. He would make me breakfast in the morning. I felt like the luckiest mom on earth.

I decided not to date. I felt very disappointed after Mark treated me that way. My feelings were hurt, and I felt every man would do the same thing. I was determined to concentrate on my son and find a better job. Everything feels so hard. I'm not sure if we made a mistake moving to Atlanta or not. It was a struggle to go from having two jobs in Ohio and bringing a decent income home and not having to worry about how to pay my rent or bills or put food on the table. Now I was living from paycheck to paycheck. I could hardly pay my bills while working forty fours a week at $12 an hour. With tax and insurance coming out, that didn't leave me a whole lot. I had to find one good job, so I didn't have to be going through this all the time.

I put on a brave face every day. At least I had a roof over my head. Some people don't even have that, and I'm grateful to God for that. Working my second job was a challenge. It was really cold, and I was working at department store as a cashier where they always had me going outside in the cold. I couldn't take it anymore, so I quit my job and started driving Uber, even though I hate driving. My son said, "Mom, how are you going to drive Uber when you hate driving?" I said it would be okay. He said, "Mom, do you think it was a mistake moving to Atlanta?" He talked about this movie that he watched and explain how the family was about to move to a different country, and the mother realized it would be a mistake to move, and they changed their mind.

I looked at him and said, "Baby, things seem hard right now, but it will get better with time. I promise it will. Don't worry. Just be happy. Your mother's got this. Okay?"

He looked at me and said okay. He hugged me and said, "I love you, Mom." I was speechless. I didn't know what to think or say to him.

It was almost Christmas, and things were still hard. I explained to him that I wasn't going to able to get him anything for Christmas. He said, "Mom, it's okay. I have everything I need." I felt grateful for having such an amazing kid. I thank God for this blessing. I have a great kid who does his homework without me even saying to do the work. He loves school.

What else can I ask for? I have it all. We go everywhere together. People think he is my brother because he is taller than me and we almost look alike. I work from 11 p.m. to 7 a.m. I would get off work and drive Uber from 7 a.m. to 12 noon. I would call to make sure Matt was awake. He would take a shower and get dress and pack his lunch for school, and he would text me and say, "Mom, I left the apartment. I will see you later. I love you." I would text back and say the same thing. I would use Find My iPhone so I knew where he was at all times. I continued to do Uber and still worked my night shift. It was hard, but I wasn't going to stop.

I decided to go to school at Paul Mitchell, and I applied for the minimum loan so I could get extra money to pay the bills. But because I came from a different country and I had my name changed before moving to the United States, my high school diploma was no good. I had to take a GED class. It was a little harder than I thought, but Matt helped me. He is really good with numbers. His favorite subject is math. He explained it and showed me how it worked. I felt blessed. He helped me with my entire class, and thank God, I passed my GED with a 2.1 GPA. I was very excited to get something accomplished while trying to better our lives.

On Friday after work, I went to do Uber. I picked someone up from Alpharetta, Georgia and drove to the downtown Atlanta airport. After I dropped him off, I decided to stay around. That was when my car broke down. Smoke started coming out of the engine. I stopped and looked. It looked very bad. I started panicking and praying, "God, please do not allow my car to break down on me." I drove to Auto Zone, hoping they could help me, and they told me what it was. They showed me a place where I could take it and have them fix it. When I got there, they said they were busy, and it could take up to five hours before they could attend to me. I couldn't wait because I hadn't slept after working the night before. I told myself God was in control, and I could try to drive little by little to make it home.

I started heading home. I had my emergency signal on, and I drove slowly. I drove at about ten mph, and the smoke was crazy. I parked on the side of the road, and I started crying because I was overwhelmed. I was not sure what to do. I had just moved to Atlanta. I didn't have any family or friends there. Who was I going to call? I wasn't sure. While I was parked on the side of the road, this guy came up to me and said, "You can't drive this car. If the smoke this that bad, the engine can be messed up."

I called my insurance company. They said to find a towing company and send them the bill. they would reimburse me later. The only person I knew was my new friend at the leasing office. I called her and told her. She said she was going to a lunch date, but that could wait. She told me to stay where I was, so I did. She came. She dropped everything she was doing and came. She came and sat inside my cold car with me and called every towing company. She said she would stay with me until they got there. I said I didn't even have the money to pay them. She said, "Give me your phone," so I did. She then downloaded Google Pay on my iPhone and transferred money into my account.

I said to her, "No, you don't have to do that."

She said "I'm here to help. Whatever you need. That is what friends do." I was shocked. She didn't have to do that, but she was there for me when I didn't have anyone else.

After we sat in the cold car for thirty minutes, the towing company showed up, and I went with them to the mechanic. They said they would call me and let me know. I took an Uber home. I felt like the world was coming to an end. I didn't have the money to pay if the car got fixed, so I put it in God's hands, hoping for the best. After two hours, I got the call, and they said it was going to cost $400. I told them to go ahead and fix it. I called my niece and friends—anyone I could think of—for help, but none of them could help me. My only hope was my best friend, Jack. I told him, and he said, "I got you. I can call them and make payment over the phone; just let them know."

I was so grateful to him, and I thank God for having him in my life for all these years. he has been my rock. It feels amazing to have such a wonderful friend to have your back and be there for you when all hope is lost. I called my new friend and told her the car could be fixed and how much it would cost me. I also told her I had found help, so I was okay. I told her how grateful I felt having her in my life and said nobody had ever done what she did for me, besides Jack. I said I felt blessed to have her around. The next morning, I called the shop to see if the car was ready, and they said yes, but the payment hadn't been made yet.

That morning, I had job orientation. I called my new friend, but I think she was sleep because it was too early in the morning. I began to walk. I was halfway there when she called and said, "Where are you?" I said I was walking. She said, "No, it is 20 degrees outside. You are going to be sick. Stay where you are. I'm coming to get you again." She saved me. After dropping me off, I picked up my car after orientation. I was confused about where it was. You begin to learn; new things will be broken. Where you begin to heal and be frustrated is where you start to make authentic decisions. Don't be sad, because if you are brave enough, you can hear your heart's wisdom through it. I know that when you just believe and pray, God will answer you. Being in Atlanta wasn't as easy as I thought. I had everything going for me back in Ohio. I had my two jobs, which paid me well. I had friends that respected me and came to me for advice. I had a big three-bedroom house. I was living my life; you could say that even though I didn't have a man. That was the last thing on my mind. It was me and my amazing son. I love this life, I said to myself.

I regret moving to Georgia. I thought once I moved here, I would find a great job, meet a wonderful man within six months of moving to Atlanta, and be in a wonderful relationship and be happy, but it was the opposite. it being hard. I was struggling more than when I was in Ohio. I had much on my mind. I was having a hard time sleeping during the day when I got off work. After I met Mark on Tinder and how he behaved, it left a bad test in my mouth. I didn't feel like dating anymore. I got comfortable in my space.

I would get upset when I would see a man and a woman holding hands. I asked myself, *Why not me?* But deep down in my heart, I wasn't sure if I wanted a relationship. Maybe the sound of it got me excited. I told myself to take things one day at a time. That is all I can do. Going back to Ohio wasn't an option for me. For the fear of my friends and family telling me "I told you so," I was not going back. I had to make it work, no matter what.

I sit back and observe every person in my life, whether I talk to them or not. I know who motivates me and keeps it 100 percent. I also know who talks about me. I know who I can trust and who I need to keep a distance from. Whether I say anything to them or not, I allowed them to be fake. Amelia always called to check on me. Our relationship wasn't great, but it was getting somewhere.

All I want is a relationship with my family. I would be happy if they pretended as if they cared for me. At least that would make me happy because my family would have my back somehow.

I don't know what it is, but as soon as I lay my guard down and start to open up to my sisters, they come at me in some way, and I go back to hiding from everyone and keeping my distance from my family. I have been criticized by my friends and family. This time, I will not allow it anymore. After my car was fixed, I started my part-time job, but it wasn't easy working two jobs and taking care of a kid. I felt bad all the time, but one of the best things about my son is that he understands me. I don't even have to explain myself. He gets it.

I continue to live my day-to-day life, even though things haven't been easy for me. I don't make enough to pay my rent, but my best friend is always there for me, no matter what. Life in the Atlanta is harder than I thought, but I'm determined to make it work.

James has been very nice to me. It was a surprise to me. He usually verbally abused me and called me names, but we began to co-parent. We started to communicate with each other about our kid. I never thought this day would come, but it is important for me to get along with James for the sake of the child and nothing more.

Every day, I am grateful to God for my life. God is the reason I'm making it. My friends always told me to look for a rich old man to take care of me, but I kept telling them no, I'm not impressed by money, social status, or job title. I'm only impressed by the way someone treats other human beings. I don't want to settle with someone because they have money. I want to be with someone because we love each other.

My friends don't understand me. They think there is something wrong with me. I told them that I'm different from everyone else. I don't like to date a guy because he is rich and I want his money. I will be with him because I want to or because of the way he makes me feel. I'm living my life the way I should, even if it is hard.

I hadn't been in a relationship in three years, and I wasn't thinking about it. I was trying to work hard and make a better life for myself and my son. That was my priority.

Each time I spoke with some of my family, I felt like they sucked life out of me. They would say something that would make very upset. They know how to push my buttons. I don't even think they care about me.

My sister said, "You only have one child, and I have four kids. Two are in college, one is in high school, and the other is in middle school, and they are in private schools." I was shocked. I couldn't believe what she was saying to me after I had just told her I thought family was supposed to have each other's back, and I didn't feel that way about mine. When Kim calls, she also pretends as if she cares, but she only calls to see if I would tell her what is going in my life so they can tell me why I'm not married and having another kid. I feel like they thought I wanted their friendship, so they used that to try to control my life somehow. I'm tired looking over my shoulder and feeling I have explain myself to them.

I wear my heart on my sleeve. I have a big heart, and that gives people around me opportunity to take advantage of me, but life has also taught me that you can't control someone's loyalty, no matter how good you are to them. It doesn't mean they would treat you the same, no matter how much they mean to you or how much you value them. They would never value you the same. Sometimes the people you love the most turn out to be the people you can trust the least.

Amelia and Kim are my sisters besides my other sister back in Ghana. She said they care about me, but I don't know anything about her or things that were going on in their lives. Kim and Amelia are very close. They share things among themselves, but they've never once shared anything with me. I'm not who they are, and each time I call, they wanted to know about my personal business. They never told me anything about them. I thought sisters were supposed to share secrets together, but with my family, nothing like that happens.

I came to terms with the fact that my family would never return the love I have for them, and from that day, I said to myself that things would never be the same again. I'm tired of being walked on and feeling like I'm nobody or my feelings don't matter. I came to a place in my life where peace became my first priority. I have deliberately avoided certain people to protect my mental, emotional, and spiritual state. I decided to separate myself from them. I avoid any call that comes from Amelia or Kim. I don't answer. I feel free. I don't feel upset, but I have peace of mind, which was what I needed. I have a voice in my head telling me what I should and shouldn't do.

I have been through a lot, but I wasn't prepared for what is happening to me in Atlanta. You can never be prepared for what is to come, no matter what you have already been through in life. I was having a hard time paying my rent. One of my friends introduced me to North Fulton Charity, where they help people in need of food and rent. My first time there, the caseworker asked me, "Do you have family?" I said yes. "Do they help you, or can they help you?"

I smiled and said family doesn't care if I make it or not. She didn't understand. I told her my only family was my son. "No, I don't have a family, but I'm sure if I become rich today, I will have a lot of family around me." She smiled.

I'm focusing on myself and my son. Things haven't been easy, but I trust in God, so I left everything in his hands. I was able to finish my GED. That was my second accomplishment, and my greatest achievement was also my first accomplishment: my son. Being a single mother wasn't easy, and I was able to raise him all by myself. Being a single mom is the most underpaid job in the world. When I look back, I'm proud of myself, because it wasn't easy. I raised the most amazing man in the world. He's kind, sweet, humble, and respectful. He's always trying to help other people. He makes sure I'm okay. He is the smartest person I've ever known. Since the sixth grade, he has made the honor roll eight times. I feel like I have done a great job so far. After everything I have been through, God has blessed me with such an amazing child. I couldn't ask for anything more. He's perfect for me.

He gives me a reason to wake up every day and keep moving. He gives me a reason not to give up in life. He gives me hope and clear mind. Some days I don't feel like getting out of bed, and he will come to my room and say, "Mom, are you okay? What is wrong?" He touches my head to see if I have a temperature or not. No matter what I'm going through at the moment, just the love he is showing me makes me feel better.

I have had so many disappointments in life, from my family members, friends, jobs, boyfriends, best friends, and my baby's dad. I realized things don't always go the way you planned. I have had setbacks and feelings of regret. I have focused primarily on the personal choices that I have made. I have made bad choices in friends and boyfriends, and places I should have been.

I hoped that by starting school, I would be able to pick up from where I left off and make a better life for myself and this amazing man in my life, my son. Starting Paul Mitchell wasn't as easy as I thought. I go to school from 9 a.m. to 5 p.m., and then I go home, cook dinner, make sure Matt does his homework, and ask him how his day was. I get three hours sleep before going to work from 11 p.m. to 7 a.m. Some days, I don't feel like moving.

I'm so tired as I sit in my car and cry. I feel like this struggle will never end and none of my family members have my back. My relationships with my sisters are the same; nothing has changed. I have learned the hard way not to trust anyone but myself. I don't depend on anyone. I don't ask anyone for anything—especially men. Once you ask, they went something in return, and I'm not willing to give anything in return for any reason.

I'm sitting here to write a good explanation for my son, so he knows never to depend on anybody, especially family, because they will let you down and never look out for you. I learned that the hard way. Each time I spoke my mind to someone my family knew, my sister Kim would call me a witch and any other name she could think of and say how ungrateful I am. My life wasn't getting any easier. I neither enjoy life the way I see it nor pain, which I have known my whole life.

Life has taught me that you can't control someone's loyalty. No matter how good you are to them, that doesn't mean they would treat you the same. No matter how much they mean to you, it doesn't mean they would value you the same. Sometimes, the people you love the most turn out to be the people you trust the least.

As I continue to live in Atlanta, life gets even harder. I don't make enough money to cover my bills. I live from paycheck to paycheck. Some days, I don't even have food in the house, and I find myself crying myself to sleep. As long I can feed my son, that's all that matters to me. Some of my new friends keep telling me it will get better with time, but I keep regretting my choice to move here because I had a great life in Ohio. Even though I was single, I wasn't worried about that.

I have two great jobs and wonderful friends who have become my sisters and have my back. I still go to school during the day and work at night. Some days I wish I had a boyfriend, and I fantasize about my dream husband and how perfect he is: God-fearing, humble, and handsome. It sounds crazy, but I do, and it helps me through my days and nights. Everyone has had a fantasy of their dream man. Every man I have ever dated made me feel like I was dating my father: a charming, handsome, smart, bad-tempered ladies' man. I dated my father over and over again until I couldn't take it anymore.

I feel like my family never hears me, and I feel like they are in denial. They didn't believe me when I spoke. They don't hear me, and they chose not to hear me because I don't matter. I was a liar as a kid. I did things I wasn't proud of. I was never perfect, and I'm still not perfect.

Moving to Atlanta has been a challenge for me. Sometimes all the bad things happened at one time, and there is nothing I can do to change that.

Life just hit me at one time. I received a call from Ghana that there was a heavy rain on my land that I bought a few years back, and all the wall blocks came down. Not only that, but a few days later, someone stole my information and used it in the amount of $300. I had my life insurance coming out.

My cell phone bill, cable bill, and storage bill were hard to pay, and the worst part was that I didn't even have food at the house for my son. We had no water and no food—not even $1 to buy eggs. I felt hopeless and defeated. I had no money in my account, and I had an overdraft, and the bank was closed because it was a holiday. I wasn't sure what to do after work. I checked my credit card and I had $10.99, so I went to Walmart and bought eggs, $0.99 juice, $1.79 milk, and two boxes of Hamburger Helper.

I made breakfast and Hamburger Helper for lunch. I took a shower and tried to sleep. As I laid down, I had so many thoughts going through my mind. I have two voices there; one kept saying, "Just give up, quit your job and school, and stay home and do nothing." The other voice said, "Don't give up; you have been through so much, and you have come far. Keep going; there is hope." I started crying, and at the same time, I began to pray to God to guide me through this difficult time. I couldn't do this alone.

I heard a knock at my door. It was my son. He said, "Mom, are you okay?"

I said, "Yes, baby."

He said, "Why are you so sad?"

I said, "I'm just tired."

He said, "Get some rest." He kissed me and said, "I love you, Mom," and left. I got even sadder, but I wasn't ready to give up, not yet. I would keep fighting through whatever life throws at me. I would be strong, I would be brave, and I would be fearless because I know I'm never alone—God is with me.

The next day, I went to title office to get a loan to pay all these bills and to get food on the table for my son. I spoke with the bank, and they disputed the charges on my card. Life was throwing every punch at one time, and everything I went through that day, God knows I can handle. He would never give you more than you can handle.

Meanwhile, I deposited money into my sister Amelia's account to buy my lotion. She said, "Where are the tax and mailing fees?"

I said, "I gave you enough."

She said, "You are not the only one who doesn't have money."

I said, "So you don't even have $20 for mailing my package? Wow, okay." Amelia has never done anything for me in my whole life. I'm not expecting anything, but as a family, we were supposed to have each other's back. I guess I was wrong. Deep down in my heart, I know better, but I think when it comes to my family, I'm always in denial. I believe what I want to believe. I always hope for the best and hope to see a change in one of my family members. I have more support from my friends than my family. It has always been like that. Until God comes, I don't believe that will change. Maybe it will, but for now, I have no control over what has been happening in my life. Sometimes with all the pain and struggle, I put on a brave face. I would take pictures and put them on social media so people would think my life was perfect and I was happy, but in real life, I'm dying on the inside.

I'm hoping for a miracle to happen. I try not to look back on my past life. It wasn't perfect, but I was happy. I wasn't worrying about my rent and my bills. I had a great job that paid for everything and wonderful friends. I called my family who really care about me, but I also gained great new friends in Atlanta who are wonderful people, so I lost one thing and gained another. You can never get it all in life.

I know how life can be hard at times, but sometimes I forget and I have to remind myself to keep pushing through it. I also have amazing friends who tell the truth that it is okay to ask for help. I never ask for help. I'm always determining to do it alone. I have always done it by myself. I hate to be the center of attention. My friends know how stubborn I am, but that works to my advantage, as I never give up until I get what I want.

My friends tell me to ask. They say, "When you ask for help, it doesn't make you weak or independent. It doesn't change anything." It makes my life easier, and I'm so thankful that I have them in my life. My friends told me to live my life with purpose and to focus on the blessings, not the misfortunes, and to focus on my strengths, not my weaknesses, and to be myself, not to wait for other people's approval. Most importantly, they say to have a positive and humble mindset no matter what situation I'm in. They say I should count my blessings, not my problems, and I will realize the beauty of life.

Everybody who reached out their hands to help me gave me disappointment and lies. They always wanted something in return. My life has become hard and harder each day. Going to school full time and working at night full time is harder than I thought. I have my good and bad days. My bad days are very bad. I cry about every single thing, either small or big.

People asked me how do I do it, going to school from 9 a.m. to 5 p.m. and working from 11 p.m. to 7 a.m. Each time, I told them I did not know, but one thing I did know is God gave me the strength to keep moving and living my day-to-day life. I just live one day at time and leave the rest in God's hands.

Some days, I feel like the world is against me; so is everyone else. I feel people are judging me, including my family and friends.

Every day when I go to school, people will say hi and smile at me, and I will say to myself that just the look in their faces makes me feel they are not sociable. The energy at the school took toll on my body. It wasn't a good feeling. It gave me the unpleasant feeling that they are not honest. From the beginning, my frustration grew more and more every day at school. School and work were taking toll on me physically, mentally, and emotionally. I felt so bad all the time. I wished I could change things, but I couldn't, and I wasn't ready to give up on life.

I had my son to worry about. I sometimes had a hard time getting out of bed. For the past few days, I had been crying all the time. I didn't want to give up, and I didn't know what I could do to make it better. I had witnessed so much disappointment in my life, and I no longer trusted or relied on people to help me with anything. I know God gave me the strength for a reason, and I can do anything I set my eye on with no setbacks. There is a reason why I'm on this earth. I would not live to forfeit it all. Working full time and going to school full time has put a toll on my body. Some days, I just cried because I couldn't take any more of the hurt, the hate, the disappointment, and the tiredness.

My best friend Jack called. He said, "Why are you crying?"

I said I wasn't crying.

He said, "I know, and I know you are crying right now." As we spoke, the cry became more than I could control, and he could really hear me cry. I said, "I'm so tired. I can't do this anymore."

He said, "You need a break. Come to me and let me baby you." We hadn't seen each other in fifteen years. I smiled. He said, "Is that a smile I'm hearing?"

I said, "Whatever."

The next day, he called with a ticket and said, "Come to Cancun."

I said, "I have school and work; I can't go anywhere."

He said, "If you don't come, you will pay me back my money for the ticket." I said fine, I would come. I took two days off work and school. I didn't care much. I just needed my best friend.

Before I knew it, I was on the flight to Cancun. When I got there, there he was with his big belly. We hugged for a long time. I said, "Why is your belly this big?" He smiled at me. I said, "You are pregnant with twins."

He smiled at me again and said, "Stupid."

I said, "Big head," and we both smiled.

Jack's wife was pregnant, so she couldn't fly. Cancun was so beautiful. It felt calm, and it was so hot it felt like 95 percent humidity. Jack said, "Why are you scared of the sun?"

I said, "I don't want to be dark."

He said, "You not white." I smiled. He had already checked in into the hotel. I said I needed food. We went to the hotel, put my luggage down, and went out.

It was the most beautiful place I had ever seen. The people were nice. We had dinner and went back to the hotel. I was tired. He was tired. He sat in bed, and we talked and talked. It felt like old times. We were up all night. I wasn't sure what time I fall asleep. The next morning, we woke up, showered, and dressed up. I went to the lobby for breakfast; they said we had to pay. I said okay, but I was taking the food to my room. They said I couldn't do that, and if I wanted the food in my room, then I should order room service. I got upset and I left. I didn't even pay for it.

Jack asked, "Why didn't you eat there?"

I said, "I don't want to."

He smiled and said, "Let's go to the beach; we can eat while we are out."

He rented a car. While he was driving, I was taking pictures. It was so beautiful. We went to the beach, and everybody was looking at me. I said to Jack, "Why is everyone looking at me?"

He said, "Because you are beautiful." I only went and walked around in the water. He said, "Swim."

I said "No, unless you want me to die. Just take pictures."

He said, "So you are here for the pictures."

I said, "What else?"

He smiled and said, "You are useless."

I smiled and said, "Back at you."

We both smiled. He left to bring the car. While I was standing, a guy come to me and said, "Can I take a picture of you and me?"

I looked at him and said, "Me?" He said yes. I said okay. I felt like a star. I took pictures with few of them. Jack called and said to come on. I told him when I got in the car. He said, "Don't flatter yourself."

I said, "Don't hate," and we both smiled. It was the best day of my life.

We went and had dinner. It was so much food for a little money. I said, "This food can feed ten people. I wish Matt was here; he would have loved it." Matt was spending summer break with his dad for the first time in a long time. "I miss him so much, and how

I wish he was here with me. it has always been always him and me against the world, just as me and Dad were."

He said, "Bring Matthew next time."

I said, "Really?" He said yes. The food was so much, so we couldn't eat all. I took the rest with us.

The next few days were okay. I didn't want to worry Jack too much, so we did much relaxing, and then I told him I wanted to go on a tour. Jack said, "You been working so hard. Please take things easy and enjoy this beautiful place." We both called each other names, and we would look at each other and laugh. The next few days in Cancun with Jack were magical; it felt like old times. I wasn't thinking about anything. I was happy for the first time in a long time.

The tour would last for twelve hours, and he said it was too much. I said, "Lazy head." He smiled. We booked it for me. The next morning, the tour car came and picked me up. There was a lady in the tour bus. She said, "Are you by yourself?" I said yes, and she said me too.

I said, "My friend was lazy, so it is just me." We started talking and talking. After a while, I realized we have so much in common and we connected so well. It was weird. She told me about herself, and I did the same thing. We hit it off right away. We went to see Chichen Itza. It was the most beautiful place I ever saw. I loved it. I was having so much fun. It felt like I had known her my whole life. I was comfortable being around her. I told her, "You don't meet people by accident, and nothing in life happens by coincidence." Unfortunately, I had to go back to the US and leave the amazing Chichen Itza.

We were dropped back off at our hotel. We got back. I told Jack I wanted to stay for another night. He didn't like the idea at first. Jack said, "Someone can steal you away."

I laughed at him and said, "You are very stupid," and he smiled at me. Jack said I could stay another night if I want to, but I wasn't sure. The next morning, I decided to go back home. I didn't have enough money, and I didn't want to spend my rent money. I told my new friend that I would be leaving the next morning. We were sad. We had so much fun.

Jack said, "Anytime you want to come back, just tell me, and you can bring Matt next time. My wife will have the baby, and we can all be together." I said okay, but I was sad to leave. I already missed him and my new friend. She and I exchanged numbers, and we continued on Facebook and WhatsApp. I felt sad. Jack and I got to the airport, and he made a joke. He said, "Stupid girl, do you remember when you left me in Ghana, and now you want to go back to the same place you left me fifteen years ago?" I smiled with tears in my eyes. He hugged me and kissed my cheek. He said, "This is not goodbye. We will see each other again."

I wanted to cry, but I was being strong. I didn't want him to see me cry. They were tears of joy and sadness at the same time. I walked through the line to check my bags in my flight. I was crying on the inside. I couldn't believe I was leaving him behind again. He was my brother from another mother. I told Jack before he left that I was going back to reality, back to my old life, going to work from 11 p.m. to 7 a.m. and going to school from 8:30 a.m. to 5 p.m. I realized I didn't like this kind of life anymore, and I needed to work hard by finishing school and having my own shop. On the flight, I missed Cancun, Mexico, but life must go on. I missed my baby so much. I became emotional. I was not sure if I was emotional about leaving Cancun or going back home or about missing my child or my best friend Jack.

Back in Cancun, I told Jack I didn't feel like dating and I was comfortable in my space. I told him I had so much going on that I don't have time to date, or maybe the idea of dating my father scares me. I don't want to babysit a grown man. Jack understands me. He was the only friend who never judged me or looked at me different. I told him that I had so much love to give, and I was afraid it would hurt once I found it. I said I have been looking for love in the wrong places and trusting the wrong people. I have a big heart. I said I was afraid that I would be hateful, and because of that, I don't want to date. I said, "Grown men act like they are kids, and I don't have time for it, but if God says I will get married one day, I will." Until then, I will not look for it. I don't even care for sex. I'm in so much pains all the time with my health problems that I don't care. I don't think about it, and I don't want it, either. Jack got me. he understood where I was coming from and where I was going when I got to the Atlanta airport.

I started to stress out. I called Jack. He said, "Don't stress out in the airport parking lot." I couldn't find my car keys. I took everything in my luggage out, not knowing it was in my small bag. I thought I was going crazy, and I went to exit. They said it cost $20 per day to park your car, and they charged me $80. I was so upset. I told Jack. He said, "It is okay. Don't worry; God will give you money in return." When I get home, it was quiet. I slept all day. I didn't want to feel anything, but once I wake up I felt lost and empty. I felt like something was missing in my life.

Being in Cancun with Jack and having someone to talk with felt good, but I was still not ready to date. Being in Cancun bought back memories. I tried to forget. Mexico looked so much I like Ghana. It was like the small town I grown up in. I saw the people and how little they have, and I saw them selling oranges and other stuff. I felt for them, and I realized that I have so much, and I need to be grateful and say thank you to God every day.

It was amazing, being with my best friend Jack in Cancun and waking up feeling loved and blessed. I know that one day I will find the man of my dreams who will love me for me. I have cried endlessly, and I have been hurt so much. Almost all my life, I have been abused physically, emotionally, and mentally. I have been sexually assaulted, and I have been look down upon and talked to like I was nobody. Each and every family member thought they broke me, but God lifted me up. Jack never looked down upon me. He loves and cares for me when no one does. Maybe one day, I will find a man just like Jack.

I know being in Atlanta hasn't been easy. I went through so many challenges and so much in life. Sometimes I feel God has forgotten about me while I've been working full time and going to school full time. I thought it would be easy. Since I moved to Atlanta, sometimes I cry night and day. I have been looking for a better job, but I have had no luck. I have a hard time understanding why I couldn't find a job, but after all that, I kept my head high and believed that God has a reason for everything he does. My son gives me the strength to keep going. Some days I don't feel like getting out of bed, but as I look at my son, I drag myself out of bed.

I can't give up, at least not yet. Maybe I can give up in the next lifetime, but not this one. Things are hard and harder. Sometime I do Uber on Saturday, so I can pay the bills. It felt like I was doing three things at the same time. I know I make mistakes and I have made bad decisions in my life. I'm still making my mistakes. That is the only way I can learn from them. God knows I'm strong enough that I can conquer the world and everything life throws at me. I have come to understand that I can't control life and can't control what happens to me, but I can live day by day and live in the moment.

CHAPTER 12

MOVING TOWARD THE FUTURE

You may think I'm crazy. I know I am to still think about my sisters, my cousins, and my friends who have hurt me too many times. I don't know how to be selfish even if I try. I miss my sister Amelia. Even when I decided not to talk to her, I just couldn't do it. I called her, and behold, she answered her phone and pretended like nothing had happened between us. Yes, this is my family. This is how they are. We pick up where we left off. I'm still trying to finish cosmetology school, but it is hard for me. I begin to fall into depression. Well, that is what I keep telling myself. Some days, I feel like I can conquer the world, and other days, it takes me three hours to convince myself to shower. I worry about things I can't control. I'm tired all the time. Sometimes, I cannot get three hours of sleep after school before work. I feel like I am failing not only myself, but also my son. When things get harder, I just look up and smile and say, "I know that was you, God. I know you are there."

There came a time when I was struggling financially. People saw me and asked how I was, and I smile and said I was doing great. Sometimes they asked, "How do you do it, going to school full time and going to work full time? When do you sleep?"

I smiled and said, "I'm doing the best I can for my son. God is in control." Then I sat in my car and cried.

This is my favorite prayer: Thank you, Father, for Your grace to stand strong no matter what I am facing in life. I choose to keep in faith. I choose to keep praying. I choose to keep believing, knowing that the victory is on the way. In Jesus' name, Amen.

I pushed myself hard because I was determined to complete cosmetology school, and also I wanted to set a good example for my son by letting him know that no matter what you are facing, you should never quit school and never give up on life. I continued to go to school during the day and work at night. My sleep schedule had not changed, but my determination was stronger than ever. God answered my prayers, and I got a new job with better pay. Things were getting better, and I had a few more weeks left to finish school. Things were getting better for me. My son was on the honor roll. He's made the honor roll seven times. He seemed happy; so was I.

My graduation day came. Nicole came all the way from Kansas City to surprise and support me. I was proud of myself after everything I have been through. I finished school and took time off to spend time with my son and rest my mind. My son got a scholarship to go to college. He also took the SAT, and he wanted to go to Duke University for a neurosurgery summer program. He wants to go Harvard University, Yale, Stanford, or Princeton in the future. He is such an amazing son. I couldn't ask for anything more. God doesn't give you more than you can handle.

Our life has changed for the bigger and better, and I am still taking things one day at a time and hoping for my happy ending soon. I don't claim to have all the answers; I'm taking life one day at a time. These life lessons are what get me through challenging times: Growth is a process. We are all works in progress. Every day is a new day to be a better person, and every day, we make mistakes and learn from them. Never allow the past to predict the future. Remember that people are human, and they will hurt, disappoint, and betray you, but keep loving and believing. The ability to love unconditionally is a gift, and the ability to love is not a weakness; it's a blessing. Love is kind, patient, and selfless. Forgive because God forgives you, pray for people who have hurt and betrayed you, and keep striving because the best is yet to come. Be led by God and keep your inner spirit, and when you need to make a change, take a leap of faith. Cry if you need to; it's a cleansing process. Sometimes you have to smile through the tears and remember the storm shall pass. Let God carry your burdens, and keep strengthening your faith, because it's your armor against the enemy. Don't let nonbelievers punk you, and remember that with God, all things are possible. I am blessed, and for this, I live with gratitude and expectancy of an even greater tomorrow. Be blessed, because the best is yet to come. If I can do it, so can you. The rest of your life is still unwritten, so keep your head high and stay blessed. I leave you with Ephesians 6:20 to 21:

For which I am an ambassador in bonds: that therein I may speak boldly, as I ought to speak. But that ye also may know my affairs, and how I do, Tychicus, a beloved brother and faithful minister in the Lord, shall make known to you all things.

CPSIA information can be obtained
at www.ICGtesting.com
Printed in the USA
LVHW032211300919
632711LV00004B/116